WRITE AN EFFECTIVE
FUNDING APPLICATION

WRITE AN EFFECTIVE
FUNDING APPLICATION

A Guide for Researchers and Scholars

Mary W. Walters

THE JOHNS HOPKINS UNIVERSITY PRESS
Baltimore

All rights reserved. Published 2009
Printed in the United States of America on acid-free paper
9 8 7 6 5 4 3 2 1

The Johns Hopkins University Press
2715 North Charles Street
Baltimore, Maryland 21218-4363
www.press.jhu.edu

Library of Congress Cataloging-in-Publication Data
Walters, Mary W.
    Write an effective funding application : a guide for researchers and scholars /
Mary W. Walters.
        p.   cm.
    Includes bibliographical references and index.
    ISBN-13: 978-0-8018-9355-1 (alk. paper)
    ISBN-10: 0-8018-9355-0 (alk. paper)
    ISBN-13: 978-0-8018-9356-8 (pbk. : alk. paper)
    ISBN-10: 0-8018-9356-9 (pbk. : alk. paper)
    1. Proposal writing for grants—Handbooks, manuals, etc. 2. Fund raising—
Handbooks, manuals, etc. 3. Proposal writing in research. 4. Research grants. I. Title.
    HG177.W35 2009
    658.15'224—dc22   2008056094

A catalog record for this book is available from the British Library.

*Special discounts are available for bulk purchases of this book. For more information,
please contact Special Sales at 410-516-6936 or specialsales@press.jhu.edu.*

The Johns Hopkins University Press uses environmentally friendly book materials,
including recycled text paper that is composed of at least 30 percent post-consumer
waste, whenever possible. All of our book papers are acid-free, and our jackets and
covers are printed on paper with recycled content.

To my family of friends,
with thanks

CONTENTS

ACKNOWLEDGMENTS

....

For inspiration, input, and encouragement, I am grateful to many people, including Tom Wishart, Heather Lukey, Denis Gauthier, Janice Lander, Olive Yonge, Larry Anderson, Yuet Chan, the anonymous outside reader at the Johns Hopkins University Press who provided such excellent suggestions for revision, and the press's encouraging and helpful executive editor Jacqueline Wehmueller.

Most especially I deeply appreciate the good counsel of my sons, Dan Riskin (PhD, Cornell University) and Matt Riskin (BComm with Distinction, University of Alberta), and their unwavering support.

WRITE AN EFFECTIVE
FUNDING APPLICATION

....

INTRODUCTION

I magine that you sit on a university committee whose charge is to dispense travel grants to researchers from various fields. For the current review, there are four applicants from the Department of Mathematics, all of whom want to attend the same international conference in Lisbon. They happen to be identical quadruplets who conduct their research together. Unable to decide among themselves who should go to the conference, they have each applied for a grant—but your committee is authorized to dispense only one travel grant per discipline.

The team of quadruplets studies linear and nonlinear stochastic differential equations—a subject with which (at least for the purposes of this example) you are not familiar. Everyone you know agrees that the sisters are impossible to tell apart, and a cursory review of their applications indicates almost identical biographical information, project budgets, and curriculum vitae. You wonder how your committee is going to decide among them.

You start to read the applications more closely. As you read the project descriptions submitted by the quadruplets, you discover to your relief that the researchers themselves have resolved your dilemma. They may be identical in almost every other way, but their writing styles are entirely different.

Quadruplet A has set down her thoughts in terms that are, in more senses than one, likely to be Greek to any non-mathematician. Terms like "Markovian switching" and "Galerkin finite-element approximations" provide the glue that holds together such statements as "$|\mu(x,t)| + |\sigma(x,t)| \leq C(1 + |x|)$" and "$V(X_1 + \ldots + X_m) = V(X_1) + \ldots + V(X_m)$." You diligently read the application through, then put it aside, hoping that someone else on the review panel will be able to explain it, or at least attest to its scientific soundness. If not, you may need to consult an outside expert.

Although the guidelines set a limit of two pages, Quadruplet B has written a four-page project description. You dutifully read it all. Dr. Q-B seems intent on convincing you of her team's stature in the field. She begins with a carefully annotated literature review, then goes on to position the Qs' work within the mathematical canon. Near the end of page four, you find a few paragraphs that trouble you. The applicant seems to be arguing that she has enjoyed fewer privileges than the other Qs throughout her academic life and that she should be selected to go to Lisbon because it is "her turn."

Quadruplet C has written only one page, amounting to a protest against the university's establishment of "arbitrary rules" such as "one travel grant per discipline per deadline." Dr. Q-C reminds the committee of the media attention that the sisters' quadruplethood has attracted to the university in general and to the Department of Mathematics in particular, not to mention their close work with the alumni office, and suggests that if the committee is not forthcoming, other universities may be inclined to be more supportive of their work.

Finally, you turn to the project description by Quadruplet D, and it's as if a curtain has been drawn back. This applicant has managed to explain stochastic differential equations in terms that you can understand, and she has shown how physicists as well as other mathematicians have applied the Qs' findings to their work. She has clearly explained how being present at the Lisbon conference could extend the team's reputation to economists—which would provide them with a critical new audience. By the time you finish reading, you wish you could phone Dr. Q-D immediately and tell her that the grant is hers so she can book her travel arrangements for the conference in Portugal.

This book provides information on a variety of topics to help you write a successful grant application. The basic principle of this book, however, is that, *all other factors being equal,* the most effectively written and presented grant application is likely to be the most successful grant application. The greater the difference in quality between two applications, the greater the chance that the better-prepared and better-written presentation will emerge on top.

And—as we have all seen happen in other contexts—sometimes a less-than-stunning project dressed in an outstanding-looking application can do considerable damage to projects that are, in their substance, of greater merit—even occasionally bumping them right off the track and out of contention. Is this fair? Probably not. But review committees are made up of human beings, and their decisions are affected by a range of subjective factors.

In defense of the reviewers, it is worth noting that they are not entirely without justification in placing some weight on the clarity and flow of the material they are evaluating, as well as on its substance. The well-written and well-edited application speaks to the organizational abilities of the applicant. It says that he or she considered the application process important enough to make the time and expend the effort to do it properly. It suggests that the individual who prepared the application is likely, among other things, to provide the funding agency with accurate reporting as the project goes along. In the example involving the mathematical quadruplets, reviewers might also assume that the best communicator in a grant competition is likely to be the best communicator at a conference. In short, a well-planned application indicates some appreciation for "how the system works."

A funding organization *is* a system, and it is part of larger systems, and as such it has many components and a range of accountabilities. All of them must be kept in mind.

Success Rates and What They Mean to You

Estimates of applicants' rates of success vary among funding agencies and depend in part, of course, on how the statistics are compiled. Reported success rates from different agencies range from lows of 10 percent to highs of 80 percent or more. However, such assessments include only those applications that are submitted and that are deemed eligible for consideration by the funding-agency administration and therefore only those applications that reach the reviewers. They do not take into account the proposals that fail to go forward from their respective universities and colleges due to quotas or concerns about quality or ethical considerations, or even because of political maneuverings. Nor, of course, do they consider those applications never completed by the applicants themselves due to procrastination, disorganization, systemic inertia, a general lack of confidence, or all of the above.

Nor do such statistics take into account that the word *eligible* is defined by funding agencies with varying strictness depending on the availability of funds. One researcher received a letter from a funding agency advising him that his application was determined to be "not eligible" because his curriculum vitae (CV), which some would consider to be merely a supporting document, was in the wrong format. Any omission or oversight relating to a specific guideline or deadline can result in rejection. Depending on the level of staff benevolence, the health of the agency's coffers and the nature of the funding agency itself, an oversight on your part may produce responses ranging from a phone call in which an anonymous voice whispers, "Psst! You forgot to sign Form 3B, Section 8. Get me a signed copy within 24 hours!" to a letter that says, "Dear Applicant: Form 3B, Section 8 was not signed. Your application is therefore ineligible for consideration. Please try again next year."

Why Are You Doing This?

As we discuss more fully in the next chapter, your perspective has a profound effect on the impression your application makes on the reviewers. We all know that preparing a solid proposal for funding takes a great deal of time—time most of us do not have. However, if you consider the effort required to do it—and do it well—to be a waste of time, not only will that attitude show in your submission, it will also constitute a missed opportunity on a variety of counts that have nothing to do with the outcome of the application process.

Obviously, you *do* want to receive the grant or fellowship for which you are applying, and it is the primary purpose of this book to help you to achieve that goal. In order for the process to be fulfilling—and for it to *reflect* your sense of fulfillment to the reviewing panel—it is helpful to keep sight of some reasons *other than those directly related to the outcome* why preparing your application with care can be valuable to you.

Whether you are learning the intricacies of grant writing at the start of your career or you are an established researcher looking to break into new funding areas or to succeed in increasingly challenging competitions, you can gain indirectly as well as directly from the application process. Even if you don't get the award (this time), here are a few benefits that will accrue to you:

1. *Experience.* Newer scholars may be reluctant to apply for funding because they feel it is pointless to throw themselves into the fray with all of those established researchers. Increasingly, funding agencies recognize this problem and have instituted formal systems whereby indications of promise are weighed more heavily than experience and credentials in the case of beginning researchers. Some agencies have even established separate funding programs for newer scholars.

   But even in competitions where there is no "farm team"

category, the experience of applying is invaluable to your career. The first application you prepare for a research grant or a fellowship is very difficult; the second is less so. By applying again and again, you become better at applying, and that experience helps to increase your chances of success in future applications. The skills you learn in developing your grant-writing abilities will also help you in other efforts—writing scholarly articles, for example, or employment applications.

2. *Clarification of your thinking.* Writing a grant application helps you think about what you are doing and why you are doing it, and about the importance of your work in the larger picture. It helps you learn how to explain your work to "outsiders." It helps you learn to think about what you are doing in a positive rather than a neutral or even negative light, which in turn helps you to feel and talk about your work with greater confidence.

3. *Networking.* Even if you do not get the grant you are applying for, your application will be read by a number of outstanding people in your field, or at least in fields related to yours, and there can be spin-off benefits to that. Your work may attract the attention of someone at another university, for example, who is interested in collaborating on a project with you or your research team, in inviting you to a conference, or in publishing an article about your work.

4. *Attracting other funding.* If you do not get the grant you are applying for but are close to the cut-off, you may get funding anyway from your university or college. Alternatively, other agencies may be interested in the same project.

5. *Feedback.* You may be provided with comments from expert reviewers on why your application did not succeed. This feedback can be useful in future applications—and in developing the research itself.

6. *Because it is your job.* Applying for grants is not separate

from your other work; it is an intrinsic part of it. You need the skills of successful grant writing to advance your academic career, and trying and failing is part of the process of acquiring skills. You also need to know how to write an effective application in order to become a role model for graduate students and others whom you mentor. Last but certainly not least in the "Because It Is Your Job" category is the fact that attracting money to colleges and universities is the responsibility of nearly every academic in the world. By contributing grant funding—and by attracting the recognition that comes with the funding you receive—you help to ensure the visibility and viability of the institution for which you work, in an increasingly competitive environment.

7. *Building a track record.* Even a small grant will enhance your CV. Some academics will not bother to apply for certain awards and even prizes because they do not see much monetary value relative to the amount of time they and others must invest in preparing the application. But even the Schofield Bursary you won ten years ago, back in your master's program, will enhance your CV. So what if it was set up by a kindly alumnus to reward outstanding spellers? If you think you might be eligible for a grant, especially early in your career, apply.

This Book Is about the Content of Your Application

Please note that the title of this book is not *Write a Funding Application*. It is *Write an Effective Funding Application*. The emphasis is on the "effective" part.

Most universities teach their graduate students about research and research design, the types of investigation best suited to various subject matter, the varieties of qualitative and quantitative research, how to build testable hypotheses, how to identify appropriate variables, and so on. Such issues relate in large measure to the focus of your research and to the field in which your scholarship is based.

This book assumes that the research project for which you are intending to request funding is constructed in a way that is completely air- and watertight. If you have any questions or concerns about the validity of the construction of your proposed project, you need to address and resolve them before you can even begin to think about how to make your application a standout. Many people find that writing a funding proposal is a great way to identify holes in a research project, allowing them to apply the appropriate caulking, but even the most extraordinary writing and the most convincing presentation cannot disguise a poorly constructed research question or hide a flimsy set of underlying arguments.

This book cannot and does not replace the need for proper research protocol. This book does not replace online and print materials explaining how to apply to specific funding agencies, either. This book is intended for all researchers in all fields who want to know how to present their material to any of those funding agencies in a way that maximizes their specific chances of success.

This Book Is Also about the Presentation of Your Application

Much of what you write when you are preparing a grant application is not about the project. It is about you. You would not walk into a job interview wearing sweat pants and a tank top, and you should not submit anything to a grants or awards competition that is not organized as effectively as you can make it—and set out in the clearest and most impressive fashion you can muster. You want to be so impressive that your "interviewers" don't even consider deconstructing your application to figure out why it works so well—they are simply carried along by your vision, your conviction, the soundness of your arguments, and your enthusiasm for your work.

They are *with you* from the first word to the last. They see why the work you have described is necessary and why you are the one to do it. "Success" is written all over you: they want to help you get where you have convinced them that you need to go. They want to be associated with the funding of your project.

By writing a truly effective funding application, you not only allow reviewers to see clearly what you intend to do and why, you also convey information about yourself and your capacity for the work that contributes to your chances of success.

You can do that with *your* funding application—and this book can help.

Putting This Book to Use

One of the best ways to make sure that your proposal is truly outstanding and receives an enthusiastic reception from the review panel is to establish a plan several months before the deadline that allows you to consider—calmly, thoroughly, and confidently—every component of what you must submit, from the agency's requirements for CV formatting, through the estimates you must obtain to complete the budget rationale, to the strength of the project description itself. Do as much of the thinking, reading, information gathering, note making, and organizing as you can do before you start to write the application. If you know all of the ins and outs of the funding program to which you are applying and know exactly what you want to say to the reviewers, you will find yourself eager, rather than reluctant, to get to the actual application when the time comes—hence, the structure of this book.

The first five chapters of *Write an Effective Funding Application* cover the all-important preparation stage, from securing any applicant-registration numbers you may need, to brainstorming points you may want to mention beyond the agency requirements so that reviewers can better understand your project, to ensuring you get your submission in on time. Chapter 6 focuses on the budget, which is central to the application and must be started early in the process but will remain an open file until the rest of the document is completed. In chapter 7 we begin the process of getting everything down on "paper" in a way that will allow the reviewers on the panel to see exactly what you intend to do and how you intend to do it, as well as to do whatever they can to help you get it done. Chapters 7, 8, 9, and 10 are the nuts and bolts of this book.

The grant-writing process cannot be imagined as a line with a beginning and an end. Instead, it must be thought of as a circle or a spiral. A funding application is either going to be approved by the agency or turned down. In the former case, the applicant will undertake the work that has been funded, then create follow-up reports to the funding agency, and then commence a new round of funding applications. In the latter case—unless the denial of funding includes a recommendation from the review panel or the agency that the application not be resubmitted, in which case some serious reevaluation needs to take place—the next step will be revision for another funding deadline. In either case, the submission of the original application is a step in a larger process. Many researchers have several funding proposals under consideration by different agencies at the same time and several funded projects simultaneously underway, which adds to the circular nature of the process. Chapter 11 is about dealing with rejection—and success. Chapter 12 is about creating a general approach to scholarly endeavor that reflects the ongoing nature of the grant-application process and considers things you can do, aside from working on specific proposals, to prepare for future applications.

No researcher or research team is ever successful with funding applications 100 percent of the time. This book is designed to make sure that when you press "submit," you are confident that you have done everything you can to guarantee your own success—leaving as little to fate as possible.

✸ *A Note for Graduate Students*

This entire book will be of immediate use to graduate students who are applying for scholarships or project funding, because the same principles apply to these applications as to applications intended to support research projects and scholarly investigations by more established academics. Nevertheless, I want to provide students at the master's, doctoral, and postdoctoral levels with specific information that is most relevant before one has begun to establish an independent research program. This information is included in notes like this one where applicable throughout the book. ▮▮

1

PREPARE THE GROUND

···

I t is often the case that when you become interested in a subject or are looking forward to a future event, your focus shifts and you begin to notice related subjects or events. If you are planning a trip to New York City, for example, you may start wondering about the locations of the streets and buildings in episodes of *Law and Order* that ordinarily you would see as mere backdrops for the action. If you are thinking of buying a new car, you are likely to become increasingly aware of vehicles in advertisements and on the street. When it is getting toward lunchtime, images and smells and even sounds remind you that you are hungry.

This principle is also true of writing a funding application, and if you choose to do so, you can put it to work in your favor. By encouraging yourself to engage in "leisure-time thinking" about your forthcoming application, you are certain to increase the strength of the final product—even if the exercise seems artificial or unappealing at the outset.

Therefore, rather than resisting all thoughts of your pending application for as long as possible, welcome any and all mental sidetracks in that direction as early and as often as you can. As you are taking the subway to work, walking across the campus, trying to tune out of a meeting, or drifting off to sleep, nudge your thoughts toward your application. You will be surprised at the useful connections and positive contributions you can come up with simply by

- *Daydreaming.* "My wife's cousin does some freelance writing for the local paper. If I ask him to proofread my application, maybe he'll propose an article to the paper about my work."
- *Fantasizing.* "If I get this grant, Professor Jones is sure to invite me to present at the conference in Fiji. If I'm successful, I'm going to email him immediately."
- *Free associating.* "This traffic jam reminds me of the way molecules of blood move past plaque buildup in the arteries."
- *Focused thinking.* "If I take that paragraph out, I will have room to mention the NASA project."

If you come up with a good idea, write it down. If you come up with a good idea in the middle of the night or while you are out on a run, *write it down as soon as possible.* Such inspirations are easily lost in the busyness of daily living, even when you are sure that they are so stunningly brilliant you could not possibly forget them. And even if you suspect that they are anything but stunningly brilliant—maybe even moving toward valueless or delusional—write them down anyway. Too many ideas are easier to deal with than too few, and a bad idea may stimulate a good one when you are reviewing your list later.

Live the Life of a Prospective Applicant

In addition to free associating and daydreaming, there are concrete things you can do on an ongoing basis to help with funding applications. You may not have time to do them all right now (or before you meet the deadline for the application you are writing now), but there will be other deadlines down the road.

A career as an academic means applying for grants until the day you retire (and possibly even afterward). You can contribute to your funding applications at an essential, fundamental level on an ongoing basis in the following ways.

- Connect with other faculty on the subject of grant writing. Raise the subject with colleagues in your discipline and related fields (or even unrelated fields) who have been successful with funding applications. Ask to see their successful applications. Most will be delighted to show them off.
- Connect with faculty in your area of research at other universities. Introduce yourself at conferences, then follow up with brief communications by e-mail. Making the acquaintance of these individuals will generally enrich your research life, and they will become part of the pool of knowledgeable people you can ask to write letters of support for future funding applications.
- Particularly early in your career, say "Yes" to academically related opportunities that will help build your CV, expand your knowledge, and increase your circle of useful contacts. At all stages of your career, take a page from the bibles of entrepreneurialism and choose, for example, which faculty and university committees you will join on the basis of the connections they can help you make.
- Identify sources of information on how to prepare a grant application, and pay attention to them. The book you are reading right now is a fine place to start. In addition, most universities and colleges offer grant-writing workshops and schedule instructive presentations by representatives from specific funding agencies. Many foundations and other funding sources include writing and submission pointers on their websites or direct you to other sites for this information. Continue seeking new sources until you can no longer read through a list of grant-writing tips or attend a workshop without learning at least one thing.
- Keep your eyes open for funding for which you may be eligible outside of the customary sources. Some awards offered by service groups, charitable organizations, or even private companies are not widely advertised. Put your research field

or area of study into an appropriate search engine, along with the word "grant" or "funding" or "award" or a similar term, and see what comes up. Some of the organizations may be inappropriate due to potential conflicts of interest or for other reasons, but others may be suited ideally to your project.

- Update your CV regularly—diarize a reminder to yourself to do this at least once every month or two. Otherwise, you are almost certain to forget a publication, a talk, or another accomplishment that is a valuable addition to your profile. (For more information on this subject, see chapter 11, "Build on Your Credentials.")

- Consider taking a course in logic (in person or online), or doing self-study in the field. Gaining some knowledge in this branch of philosophy can be extraordinarily useful not only for the development of funding applications but also for writing journal articles, program proposals, speeches and presentations, Web pages, and many other projects. (I say more about why logic is important in chapter 4, "Organize Your Application.") Logic is not a talent that some people have and other people do not have. Logic can be learned, and your facility with it can always be refined in order to maximize your ability to deploy it strategically when making academic arguments and building tight hypotheses.

Win from the Starting Gate

Before they complete the first line on their applications, many grant applicants have already given up hope. They may be steeped in negative statistics relating to success rates in their disciplines, geographical regions, or genders. They may dwell on rumors they have heard about the types of individuals who are appointed to the review committees of specific agencies, or they may still burn from previous rejections. Whatever the cause, their negative attitudes are reflected in their applications—with predictable results.

As the pop psychologists and consultants who frequent prime-time television and write best-selling books are always telling us, if you want to be successful at what you do, you need to take responsibility for creating that success. You need to get your head together on the topic of your future path and what you can do to improve its quality. For you as an academic, this means, among other things, that you need to take charge of your own funding applications.

Build Confidence

Most people at the early stages of their careers lack confidence in some areas relating to their work, but researchers at all stages can feel their confidence falter when they face increasingly intense competition or move into a new field. It is easy to assume that all of the other applicants in the competition are superior individuals with far more worthy projects. This is not true, of course. Some of those others probably do have "better" projects than yours, but some of them do not. By submitting an outstanding application, you can improve your chances of success considerably.

The first and most important factor in an effective funding application is your attitude toward the task. One component of the preparation of your proposal over which you do have control is your approach to it, and by controlling your attitude you can maximize the control you have over the outcome. If you do not feel confident, you need to do what it takes to feel that way.

Later in this book you will find suggestions for getting yourself into the right mind-set to actually write the grant proposal, but even before that you have the opportunity to build the necessary bedrock for confidence—by becoming knowledgeable about every relevant aspect of the proposal, as early as you can. Knowledge is the foundation upon which confidence is built. (Note that the word *relevant* is operative here, because you do need to set limits. Acquiring knowledge is a popular pastime for procrastinators, some of whom indulge in so much background work they never get the application done.)

Build Confidence by Building a Team

Many successful researchers make it a practice to assemble teams that meet well in advance of the funding deadline to help plan the writing of a grant proposal. In addition to the researcher or group of collaborating researchers, such teams can include specialists whose skills will be needed during the research, such as computer programmers and technical experts in other fields. Such teams may also include people who will only be part of the grant-planning process, after which they will fall away like rocket boosters on a space shuttle—for example, scholars with experience in writing success-ful funding applications for specific agencies, experts in reviewing budgets, grant-proposal editors, and people charged with taking notes during the preliminary meetings.

It is essential to include on your planning team technical experts who have strong skills in areas that are clearly not your specialty but are fundamental to your research—data analysts, for example, or individuals who are proficient in the use of some specific measure-ment tool or computer program that you will need to use to carry out your work. It will also be important to mention these individu-als in your application, in order to demonstrate your capacity to do what you say you are going to do; by including them in the planning right from the beginning, you will bring these people on board with your project and will at the same time strengthen your ability to write about their future contributions to your work. If they are being paid to consult, do not forget to add their fees or salaries into your budget.

Once you have your team assembled, you will see that you really do have access to all the tools you need to carry out your research successfully, which in turn will build your confidence for the writing of your grant proposal. However, this team will serve a further pur-pose. When you convene the first planning meeting of this group, you will be forced to focus—in front of others—on the reality of your funding-application deadline. This will externalize the job ahead of you, taking it from your personal to-do list out into the public arena. After the first meeting, during which you will outline your goal (getting the most fantastic proposal possible written by a specific date) and establish a series of deadlines for yourself and others, you are likely to find that the group turns into a team of coaches and supporters. Whenever you run into team members subsequently, they will want to know how you are doing on the development of your application, whether they can do anything to help, when the next meeting will be held, and so on. In short, they will serve as external manifestations of your conscience (except that they will normally treat you much more gently than your conscience ever does).

Business leaders know the value of taking a team approach to the launching of programs or projects. When they decide on an initiative they would like to incorporate into their existing operations, they call a meeting of appropriate members of their staffs and relevant outside experts (e.g., a web designer, a lawyer, an architect). They introduce the idea to the group, brainstorm, divide up the work and establish a schedule for future meetings at which they will reevaluate, fine tune, and reassess. In this way, group members are encouraged to take ownership of the vision that was conceived by the executive, and they become part of the team that helps to bring it to reality. Enlisting the moral and physical support of an outstanding group can be of great value at all stages of a research process as well.

Where Is Your Line in the Sand?

Sometimes it helps to improve your confidence about what you know, and what you want to do with that knowledge, to consider what you will *not* do. For example, if it would increase the likelihood of your project's being accepted by a review panel, would you agree to alter it? By how much? Along which parameters?

Try inventing questions relevant to your field of study, along the following lines.

- Would you be able to proceed with your work if your budget were cut by 10 percent? By 30 percent? By 50 percent? At what point would you need to turn down the funding?
- Let us say that you want to conduct a study into the incidence of newly retired individuals being hired to work as consultants for their former employers. You have assumed an age of retirement of sixty-five. You notice that a scholar who sits on the panel that will review your application has just published an article urging mandatory retirement be lowered to sixty. Would you alter your wording—or the project itself—to accommodate this viewpoint?
- You like working alone. You hate depending on other people. You realize that 90 percent of the projects funded by this agency in the past two years have been collaborative projects. Do you rethink?

Conjuring and answering such questions helps you draw the line over which you will not step. On this side of that line lies your confidence.

When All Else Fails, Fake Confidence

There are times when everything you do fails to shore up your spirit and your spunk. When that happens, you need to ask yourself a different set of questions—such as, "How *would* I talk or write about this project if I were totally confident of my position in my field? What facial expression would I have? What body posture? How would I move as I walked up to the podium to talk about my work, or sat down at the computer to begin to write, if I knew the track I was on was exactly right—and, furthermore, unique and brilliant?"

If you have done everything you can to extend your knowledge, but you are still finding that your confidence has gaps, then what you need to do is imagine how total self-assurance would affect your posture, attitude and tone—and then you need to fake it.

WHEN YOU NEED TO IMPERSONATE SOMEONE

From time to time one of the less senior members of a research team is asked to draft one of the sections of a funding application. In this situation, the writer not only needs to present an aspect of the research project in the best light possible from the perspective of the funding agency and its reviewers, he or she also needs to do it in a way that represents the perspectives, knowledge, and style of the principal investigator and/or the research team as a whole. This task can turn into an immobilizing challenge, since the two audiences who are going to review the material may be utterly different.

Being charged with a responsibility of this nature does have its advantages in terms of the grant-writing experience it offers and the feedback the more junior colleague is likely to receive. If you find yourself in this situation and fear a writer's block, the best approach is to ask as many questions as you can think of before starting—keeping in mind that knowledge is the best defense against procrastination. Make sure you know how long your segment is supposed to be, exactly what aspects of the project it is expected to cover, where in the proposal your section is going to fit and, if appropriate, what underlying principles are being stressed in the application as a whole that also should be emphasized in your particular section.

Although the principal investigator or the research team undoubtedly does not want you to use the assignment they have given you as an opportunity to showcase your literary acrobatics, every sentence that ever goes down on a page exhibits a style and tone that says something about its writer, and will therefore vary depending on whether the individual writer is self-important or modest, verbose or succinct, generally relaxed or tense, generous or selfish, and so on. If you have concerns about getting the "voice" of the lead investigator right, you can take a page from a fiction writer's handbook and kick-start the process by pretending to be the individual whose voice you are attempting to evoke. I do not mean that you should impersonate that person literally, of course, but rather that you should do so in your mind's eye. If you imagine yourself as that other person, soon you will find yourself making useful decisions that reflect your awareness of his or her writing style. You will tell yourself, "No. He would never say it this way," or "She would add a comment here about her previous work."

❧ *A Note for Graduate Students*

Some students claim (often correctly) that they could earn as much by working for an hourly minimum wage as they spend preparing a funding application. This is especially discouraging when the odds are that the application over which they have toiled for so many hours will not even be forwarded from their university to the major funding agency for which it was intended.

Others feel that those whose families can afford to pay for their graduate education should leave the scholarships for those who really need them.

Scholarships and research grants are not welfare or social-assistance programs: they exist to reward and nurture excellence in scholarly investigation and academic thought.

At this stage in your career, you have made it over whatever hurdles were required to get yourself into (or through) graduate school, which means that you have earned the right to be doing the work you are doing—which in this case includes applying for research funding or scholarship support. Creating a good proposal is not separate from the other scholarly work you are doing; it is an intrinsic part of it. Furthermore, winning smaller awards now will help you to attract larger awards that you may want or need in future.

In short, these initial attempts serve as valuable experience and may even add to your credentials. They deserve your full attention. ∎

2

PLAN AHEAD

. . . .

I f you are tempted to leave everything relating to your funding application until the last few days before the deadline—because you work best under pressure, let us say—you might just want to take a moment to look at the big picture.

You, an individual researcher and scholar at the University of X, are about to submit a very limited number of pages of information to a group of six or seven expert reviewers from other institutions of higher learning across the nation, most of whom likely do not conduct research in your specific field or in one another's. In those few pages, you must explain to this group what you are doing, why you are doing it, why you need to be doing it, and why you are the best person in the country, if not the best on the planet, to be doing it. Your submission will compete for attention with several hundreds of others, and your reviewers will probably have been reading dozens of applications each day in preparation for their meeting. In order to be considered seriously at that meeting, much less emerge as one of the successes, your proposal needs to present a lot of material logically and in clear, simple, and precise language. It will need to be a true standout.

If you want to secure a grant, you do not have the liberty to write at length or to present your ideas in anything less than the most organized fashion possible. As we all know, it takes far longer to write less on a subject than it does to write more. The process of applying successfully for a grant is not well suited to "pulling an all-nighter," even metaphorically. To do a superlative job with the requirements and restrictions the granting agency has imposed on you is likely to take not days or weeks, but months.

Start Early

(Note: If it is too late to start early, you should now skip forward to chapter 7.)

First, decide what you need to do or can do before you can start writing your application. What materials must you gather in advance in order to do the job completely and thoroughly? Most people know that it would be foolhardy to submit an application without a specific required document—your updated CV or that of one of your collaborators, for example. It is less obvious but equally true that if you update your CV before you even start the application, and therefore you know that it is done—and done properly—and will not need attention at the last minute, even this small achievement can increase your confidence and thereby indirectly improve your application. Conversely, if you begin to realize as you are refining the text in the body of the application that you will need to do a slapdash job on a CV update because you are running out of time, your concerns may undermine your optimism, and that can affect the outcome of the entire application.

Here are some of the documents and issues you might want to get organized before you start writing the text of your proposal:

- your updated CV (This may be a standard form established by the funding agency that needs to be reviewed and updated online, or perhaps your existing CV needs to be entirely reorganized or cut to a specific length in order to conform to the agency's requirements.)
- names, addresses, and CVs of your collaborators
- write-ups about industry or community partners, and names and addresses of your contacts at those organizations
- information about prospective expert reviewers if required,

Two categories of letter of intent are sent to funding agencies: one could be described as exploratory and tentative, the other as definitive and binding.

The Exploratory Letter of Intent, or Letter of Interest

Some agencies ask grant seekers to submit a letter of intent—an expression of interest in applying—in advance of the actual application. Essentially mini-proposals, the letters are meant to save you and the agency time and effort. Restricted in length, often to a page or two, the letter summarizes your project, explains how it fits with the agency's guidelines, and provides other preliminary information. You may also be asked to include a timeline and a budget. Frequently, this exploratory letter of intent is reviewed by administrators rather than by expert reviewers. These people will understand that you have not investigated the project so extensively that you are able to provide final details and costs down to the last cent. However, your letter should be as focused as possible and show that you have spent significant time and effort thinking about how you will carry out the proposed research.

One situation where a letter of intent may be invited or required is for a particularly large, complex, or multidisciplinary project. In such a project, it is of value to the applicant to make certain—before going to all the trouble to prepare a full application—that the agency agrees that the applicant is applying to the right funding program at the right time.

Where such letters are optional, it is worthwhile to submit them if you have the time. The feedback you receive can provide you with useful guidance as you write the application, prevent misunderstandings that could derail your submission during the review process, and give you confidence that you are on the right track.

The Binding Letter of Intent, or Statement of Intent, or Preliminary Proposal

For certain major funding programs or grant programs that have been established to address unique research questions, the letter of intent is much more than a simple expression of interest for the sake of determining eligibility. Here, specific requirements are carefully set out by the funding agency, and the statements are submitted to a panel of experts for review. Approval of such statements constitutes a significant endorsement that goes a long way toward ensuring that the project ultimately receives funding. Formal "invitations to submit" may be issued to candidates on the basis of successful preliminary proposals, and in some cases money may even be allocated to offset some costs in developing the final submission.

Statements of intent are more extensive than letters of interest. Essentially equivalent to the "proposal" components of other applications, they require detailed explanations of the research questions, extensive analyses of the literature, descriptions of the research methodologies, anticipated outcomes, budgets, and so on. Letters of intent can lead to the ultimate success or failure of the project and should be developed with the care and attention that their potential impact on your research and scholarship program deserves.

---

including their full names, addresses, and other contact information requested by the agency; some agencies also request names of experts in your field whom you do *not* want to review your proposal, due to reasons such as conflict of interest

- names of writers of letters of support, if any (see "Choose Your Supporters with Care," next page)
- required documents relating to ethics, protection of human or animal subjects, environmental-impact issues, proprietary information, and so on
- any required letters of support or acknowledgment from faculty or administrators in your department, college, or university

Some agencies require you to register online in advance of submitting a funding application. Their preconditions for approval can involve additional paperwork, such as getting your home institution to update its accreditation with the agency, or providing personal documents. Make sure you understand the protocols, and fulfill them ahead of time.

Find the Fit

Another step you need to take before you actually put pen to paper is to spend some time considering the nature of the funding agency. What does it do? What is its purpose? How does its mandate differ from those of other funding agencies? In the case

Choose Well . . .

The credentials and stature of the individuals you name as prospective reviewers and writers of letters of support will be noticed and carefully considered by the agency and its expert review panel. Check agency guidelines for any specific recommendations in regard to these individuals, and then spend a few minutes brainstorming a list of all the people you can think of who might contribute to your application. Do this each time you apply for new funding—do not rely on the same names you have used in the past just because it is easier. Think of people you have met and talked to at conferences in the past year or so, or people whose work has recently been published.

Once you have created a list, objectively examine the credentials of each candidate. A restrained but positive assessment of your work by a Nobel prize-winning researcher in your field will weigh more strongly in your favor than will a gush of enthusiasm from a junior colleague. When you are deciding among prospective supporters with very similar qualifications, you need to take into account such factors as geography, politics, seniority, and gender.

If you choose carefully, you can also use your outside experts to make up for gaps you cannot address directly. For example, if your university does not have a reputation for excellence in research (in your field or generally), it is a good strategy to ask for support from someone located at a university that does.

If writing a letter is going to be one of the responsibilities of your supporters, you may wish to consider their ability to write an effective letter. Many excellent applicants suffer because the recommendation letters they have solicited are opaque, long-winded, or lack enthusiasm; a carelessly written letter can doom your application, perhaps quite unintentionally on the part of the letter writer. Clearly, it is not appropriate to write the letter of support yourself, but referees usually welcome some guidance from you on the elements you would like them to keep in mind or to address as they compose a letter on your behalf. It is wise to make such suggestions gently and respectfully, saying, for example, "Here are a few points you may wish to consider mentioning if you feel it is appropriate." (For further information on *writing* effective support letters, please see appendix C.)

. . . and Choose Well in Advance

It is courteous to ask colleagues and senior university administrators as far as possible in advance of your deadline if they will write a letter on your behalf. The same courtesy applies to asking whether they will allow their names to be included in your application as potential reviewers. In the case of outside referees—people you don't see every day—you may need to ask more than one person before you find the candidate for your project. You may send an e-mail asking for a letter of support, hear nothing back, wait an appropriate length of time, follow up with a phone call—only to find that person is climbing Everest and is not expected back until midsummer.

Even if you secure the assistance of your first-choice reviewers the first time out, they are unlikely to complain that you have contacted them too far in advance. In fact, they are likely to feel even more positively about you if you have asked for their support well ahead of the deadline. This positive feeling will be reflected in their recommendation of you. Another advantage that you create with a long lead time is that if you need to follow up with a reminder after a week or a month or so, the onus of responsibility has shifted to them to get it done. If they accept your invitation to write a letter of support eight weeks before the deadline, they cannot, even in their own minds, say that you have unexpectedly added to their burdens at the last minute. If you are concerned that they may forget to write the letter, offer to send a reminder memo on an appropriate date closer to the deadline, and then do it.

of large agencies such as the National Institutes of Health (NIH), you may also need to determine which of several grant programs is most appropriate to your project, considering such factors as the particular stage of your research as a whole, and even of your overall career. Even if you are a highly experienced researcher, if you are applying to a new agency or program, you will need to consider how the program requirements differ from those you are familiar with. In cases where the agency and program are the same, you will still need to determine whether any guidelines have changed since your last application.

When you begin the application process—having so far only made the decision to apply—the money to be awarded might as well be in a locked box in a cavern one thousand precarious steps up a slippery slope from where you are right now. There is no point in setting out in your dress shoes with a bottle of water and hoping for the best. You are much better off to learn before you go—by reading and talking to other people—what the nature of the challenges ahead of you might be. The more you know, the less forbidding the task will seem, and the greater will be your chances of successfully overcoming each of the obstacles you face.

Find out what the funding agencies want. Read their websites. Go to any orientations that are offered at your university or college about specific funding programs. If possible, phone or e-mail the administrative staffs of granting agencies directly, and obtain information regarding not only the application process but also the types of projects that have been funded recently. Senior staff members who have been present during previous committee deliberations may give you their opinion about how your project compares to typical submissions and may even suggest aspects of your project that might put you at a disadvantage. Reviewers who have served on previous committees and members of standing review committees can also provide this kind of feedback.

Get as much information as you can about such agency-related issues as:

- the specific grant for which you are applying
- whether simultaneous submissions to other agencies are permitted
- the review process that the agency uses, and who has served on its reviewing panels in the past
- current reviewers (Some agencies list members of standing committees on their websites.)
- projects the program has funded in the previous two or three years
- procedures and conditions and areas of focus that have recently been introduced by the agency (Recent changes to the process are frequently highlighted in bold or red text on agency websites, and are located near the top of the list of guidelines.)
- the source of the agency's funding, to whom it reports, who decides who is on its reviewing panels, and other administrative details

In addition to tapping into the agency's own resources, search for media coverage of recent awardees and information about the agency's funding programs.

A Two-Way Fit

As you are reviewing material relating to the agency, you need to think about how to put the information to work for you. Consider to whom the board of the funding institution is accountable, immediately (e.g., government or a private funder) and in the larger picture (e.g., the public). Note any specific emphases of the funding agency—on extending knowledge to educators, for example, as in the cases of the National Science Foundation (NSF) and the National Endowment for the Humanities (NEH), or translating research findings into practice, in the case of the NIH—so that you are able to show how your project fits within the organization's mandate.

In addition, particularly in the case of smaller funding agencies, you should think about particular ways in which your project will appeal to the agency, or even contribute to its public profile. If, for example, you are applying for an award named in honor of an individual whose life was devoted to the potential contribution of civil engineering to international relations, point out how your work supports that vision.

Carefully considering the mandate of the agency or the particular

READ WITH A PEN

Read the agency's application guidelines closely. Do not merely skim the document to find out what hoops you must go through in order to submit your application. Read the explanatory text for specific actions you can take, as well as to gain a sense of the mission and philosophy of the agency. Don't simply access funding guidelines online; take the time to print them out and review them with a highlighter and pen in hand.

funding program, and your fit with it, is crucial if the funding organization is charged with addressing a specific issue, and especially if it has called for proposals on a specified subject or in a particular area. Note that, particularly in the case of small private funding agencies, such directives can be highly politically charged, and it is wise to become familiar with the source of the directives in order to evaluate whether a proposal in your area of investigation is likely to meet with a positive reception—or sometimes even whether you want to be associated with the funder.

There is no point in wasting your time or the time of the funding agency's staff and reviewers if there is no possibility of success for your project. On the other hand, a bit of fine-tuning and adjustment to a grant proposal can sometimes illuminate (or create) a fit where none was apparent before.

Know Your Field

It almost (but not quite) goes without saying that you need to become familiar with the current literature in your field of study. This is another step to take early in the application process. You need to make sure you know what is going on "out there" not only for your own sake but also so you can make it clear to the review panel how your project differs from all the other projects in your immediate area of research, and how the work of other researchers complements your own. Make a habit of taking brief notes when you read articles about research that relates to yours, and keep those notes in a file where you can find them when it is time to prepare a funding application.

Trends in research occur in every discipline. As a result, several applications at a single adjudication may sound as if they propose to do exactly the same thing—frequently something that has already been done at least once. An example in recent years is a proliferation of studies to find out why patients do not follow medical advice that they know will improve their health. Aside from the fact that most agencies are not legally permitted to fund exactly the same project twice, a host of variations on the same study can give a poorly prepared applicant all of the appeal of last week's donuts. Reviewers are likely to throw their hands in the air and say, "Not another one!"

You need to know if a dozen other researchers are working on the same topic as you are for scholarly reasons, and you also need to know so you can explain to reviewers exactly how your project differs from everything else that is out there, and why it therefore merits funding.

Establish a Plan and a Time Line

Even those who are not deliberately postponing their funding applications until the last moment often fail to schedule enough time in advance to do an outstanding job. Many people, for example, schedule a week or two for work on a grant application and tell themselves to relax and not worry about it until then. There are several problems with this approach. The time period you have set aside begins to loom on your horizon, increasing the likelihood that when it arrives you will procrastinate. Preparation and knowledge can increase your confidence and your enthusiasm for writing your application. (Confidence is to procrastination as Raid is to insects.)

If you are teaching and your funding deadline falls within the summer months, it might be tempting to leave the application until the end of term. Instead, schedule yourself half a day at least three or four months in advance of the deadline and make a list of the documents you need to gather, people you need to ask for letters of reference, and so on. Then, establish a schedule.

You need time to procure letters of support and accumulate required documents, and you need time to focus exclusively on the text component of your application (often referred to as the "narrative"). In regard to the narrative, allow time for:

- writing and editing several drafts. The first draft is the most difficult one to write, so give yourself at least a weekend or even several days of uninterrupted time when you can focus, gather all your materials, and give this phase of the writing your concentrated effort. Schedule this time for at least three months before the deadline. (Detailed information on preparing the various drafts of an application can be found in chapters 7, 8, and 9.)
- obtaining any necessary ethical reviews
- soliciting and receiving feedback from an expert reviewer. It is of value, particularly early in your career, to seek the assistance of someone among your circle of colleagues who has an informed perspective on the granting process but has not previously seen your application. This step of proposal development is also useful whenever you are entering unfamiliar granting territory. Preferably your expert reviewer will be a scholar in a discipline related to yours but not someone in the same field, and ideally he or she will have experience as a member of the kind of review panel to which you are submitting.

Note that you are not looking for anyone who delights in quibbling endlessly over details, or considers himself or herself to be a wordsmith. Explain to your colleague that you are not looking for a close editorial reading—you will be obtaining that kind of input separately—but that you are looking for the type of scholarly reading a reviewer on a funding panel is likely to give your application. You want to know whether your research proposal appears to be academically sound—whether there are questions you have left unanswered, passages that might be confusing, or gaps you may have overlooked.

Also note that, in order to be of value, this expert review needs to be done after *you* have done as much work as you can on your application.

- soliciting and receiving input from at least one skilled and objective editor or proofreader who has not previously seen your application. This must be done after you have completed your initial draft of the proposal and made it as complete as possible. (Details on identifying and using editorial assistance are included in chapter 9.)
- considering and then incorporating the feedback from the expert reviewer and the editor.

Some granting agencies offer to review draft proposals, as do some universities and colleges. Some universities and research institutes also *require* that funding applications be officially reviewed before they are submitted. If you want or need to take advantage of such services, you must build these institutions' deadlines into your schedule. Find out well in advance when those deadlines are.

Be as generous as possible when establishing your timelines—everything is likely going to take longer than you think it will. However, there also has to be some cohesion to the process. If you start too far in advance you will never be able to maintain momentum, and if you lose momentum you are likely to end up doing everything at the last minute anyway.

You also need to have alternative plans so that if someone or something prevents you from completing a certain stage of your schedule by a specified date, you can still move forward. No response by November 1 from the health unit you had hoped would provide you with your sample population? Don't wait any longer: contact the backup unit. It appears that officials are not going to get you a signed document before the deadline? Try to obtain written confirmation from someone in authority that the process for procuring the document is at least under way.

Recognize Your Power

Support your sense of confidence by remembering what *you* can control in this process. For example, one funding agency, in providing information to prospective applicants for graduate-student scholarships, indicates that applications are to be weighed as follows: 60 percent track record, 30 percent research potential, and 10 percent communication skills (based on such indicators as the presentation of the application). This breakdown might lead applicants to assume that only 10 percent of the final score depends on the quality of their applications.

Let us consider the situation from the reviewers' perspective. The most significant way for them to discover the applicants' research potential is to read the applications—in other words, to read *what* the applicants told them and to consider *how* they told them what they told them. This puts at least another 10 percent in the applicants' "communications skills" basket, which means that they are now in charge of 20 percent of the outcome. Sixty percent is based on academic background, which the applicants can do nothing to improve once they have applied. But the maturity and confidence they show in presenting their knowledge, plans, and goals will go a long way toward smoothing away any rough edges in the "background" category in the reviewers' minds. The 20 percent has now increased to 30 percent or more.

Most agencies set out criteria against which proposals will be measured by peer-review committees. These lists include such elements as innovation, potential impact, research approach, and investigator qualifications. At this stage, many applicants turn over to the agency the power for the outcome of the funding application: they assess their own ability to measure up to each of the criteria and find themselves wanting in at least one area. Consider, though, that it is not merely the content but also the clarity and confidence with which the content is presented that helps reviewers to make informed decisions. Rather than thinking of your proposal as needing to measure up to a preset list, focus on the fact that your project is a vital and viable initiative and that your job is to explain to the expert reviewers why it is unique, special, and deserving of funding—using the list the agency has provided.

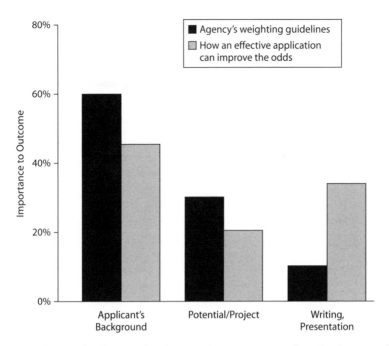

An effective funding application can increase an applicant's chances of success. The agency's weighting guidelines are from the Canada Graduate Scholarships Program: Master's Scholarships, Evaluation Criteria, www .sshrc.ca/web/apply/program_descriptions/fellowships/cgs_masters _e.asp#5.

In short, usually applicants have more control over the destinies of their funding applications than they realize they have. Careful strategizing and an investment in long-term planning can bring significant results.

✦ A Note for Graduate Students

As a graduate student or postdoctoral researcher, you are likely conducting your work in the context of the research program of a more established scholar. While this is a necessary step in the evolution of your career, you also need to keep in mind that you are building—and need to take responsibility for—your own future by making sure that the significant steps you take now contribute to what you want to do in years to come.

Not every research project with which you are associated will be directly related to the work you intend to pursue. However, there must be a clear connection *in your mind* between any research funding or scholarships for which you apply and the larger picture of your graduate program as a whole—and the purpose of that graduate program in attaining your career goals.

Know how the work you are doing as a graduate student is feeding your own intellectual interests. The ability to connect your personal interests and goals to the work you are doing now helps to build your confidence, which in turn leads to a stronger funding application. ▌

3

ZOOM IN, ZOOM OUT
Putting Your Work in Context

··

I n a first-year English course, I wrote and submitted an essay that
analyzed John Donne's poem, "The Flea." It was obvious to me
that the poem was written from the perspective of a man who
was speaking to a woman he loved and wanted to make love with,
and I proceeded to explain the poem on the basis of that assumption. However, I never directly *said* that the speaker of the poem was
a young man and that he was writing to a young woman he was hoping to seduce. Although the points I made about the poem could
not have proceeded from any other basic assumption as far as I was
concerned, and although my professor seemed to find my observations about the poem to be of merit, I was docked significant points
for not having described anywhere in the essay the basic relation-
ship between the narrator and the person he was addressing.

That experience taught me a lesson that has stood me in good
stead during all of my writing and editing since, which is to *state
the obvious*. Grant applicants are well advised to take this lesson to
heart.

You have likely been working on the specific project for which
you are applying (and toiling away in your field generally) for so
long that you have established certain principles on which you
build your every move, principles that may or may not be givens
for—or may or may not even cross the minds of—those who will read

your application. If your work involves assessing the effectiveness of various materials used as barriers in the prevention of contaminant seepage from mine tailings, it will be helpful to point out to reviewers how those contaminants, when released, impact the environment—and why, therefore, your research is important. If you are investigating the evolving characteristics of the English language during the nineteenth century, place your work into the historical, sociological, political, and comparative linguistic contexts that give your findings their meaning.

"So What?"

First, identify what basic principles and assumptions you need to clarify for readers. Then stand back and take a long look at your project from an outside, objective viewpoint. Such a perspective can help to remind you why you are doing the work you are doing. What got you interested in the first place? Who will benefit from your findings, and how? Does what you are doing have the potential to impact humanity, even on a small scale? Take some time to ask yourself questions such as these, write down your responses, and incorporate them where appropriate into your funding applications.

The significant question in this context is, "So what?"—and you need to be absolutely sure that everyone who reads your application sees that you have asked yourself that question and answered it. People who review research proposals say that many applicants do a poor job of explaining how their work fits into the larger scheme of things. Here are some specific aspects of that question to consider.

- How and where in your application will you indicate how your project fits within the larger picture in your discipline—and within your specific subfield? You need to interpret the literature review to help reviewers understand not only what research has come before this point in your specific area but also what related initiatives are going on right now that may complement the work you are doing.

- (If relevant) how does your project connect with *other* subfields inside your discipline and with subfields *outside* your discipline?

- How does your present work relate to what *you* have done before? This is always an important question and is particularly so if you are moving into a completely new area or even moving in a slightly new direction with your research, starting a collaboration with someone working in another field, or making use of a new technology or approach. Take the reviewers by the hand: show them how you got from A to B, and why.

  Knowing how to explain clearly how your project fits into your own overall program of study is of increasing importance, because some funding agencies now only fund projects within ongoing research programs—they do not fund stand-alone projects. In truth, very few projects truly do stand alone; misunderstandings in this area usually arise because applicants fail to explain how their projects fit with other work that they have done.

- How does your project connect to the objectives of the granting program? This question has special significance when you are applying to funding agencies that are attempting to establish boundaries among themselves and avoid overlap. Especially in such areas as the health sciences versus the social sciences (e.g., nursing projects in inner-city communities), or medical versus nonmedical scientific research (e.g., the use of X-rays in detecting breast cancer), if you do not know or do not clearly state why your application belongs with the agency to which you have submitted it, you may be denied funding for a reason that is not even directly related to your work.

It can be useful to embed the wording of the funding program's requirements in your application. You might rephrase the guidelines slightly, or even include them word for word within quotation marks. You want to show the direct connection between what you are doing and what the granting agency wants. The guidelines might state, "Grants in this program will be awarded only to projects that include significant amounts of research training. Research training normally involves (a) and (b) and (c)." You can say something like, "This research reflects the agency's emphasis on training future researchers in that (a) and (b) and (c) are included in the project."

In the Shoes of the Reviewer

Now that you have moved far enough outside the project to gain a useful perspective on it, take one more step and imagine the reviewing process from the panelists' point of view. One estimate says that each application typically has four minutes of a committee member's time to demonstrate its value and the value of the applicant's research. Use your four minutes wisely.

Reviewers receive a large box of applications—as many as two hundred—six to eight weeks before they are scheduled to meet and discuss them. Given all the other commitments such individuals have as academics and as human beings, this means that when they read the applications on their own, they may need to review between ten and twenty submissions at a sitting. They are likely to read applications during their evenings and on weekends, when they would rather be doing something else, or under less than ideal conditions—on airplanes, for example. They may even be tired and irritable.

Reviewers can tell within the first couple of paragraphs whether an application is viable or not. Given the circumstances under which the reviewers are reading applications, you must assume that they are going to set your application aside if it does not immediately appear solid or viable. One seasoned reviewer said, "If the first paragraph doesn't grab me and hold me, you have lost me." While most reviewers will give most applicants at least a page, your goal is to keep the reviewer reading to the end.

Most review panels are composed of intelligent people who are highly regarded for their expertise. The members of many panels represent a range of areas within a field or a discipline, and some panels are interdisciplinary. Assume that some or all of the panel's members are working in slightly different areas than you are, and find out, if possible, who sits on the panel that is likely to review your work. The nature of the granting agency, and whether its funding programs are interdisciplinary or discipline specific, provide clues. If the latter, find out how discipline specific the programs are. Consult any lists you can find of current and previous reviewers. What are these panelists sure to know? What might they *not* know? What are they *likely* not to know? When in doubt, it is wise to assume that your audience will know nothing about your specific area, and that you need to tell them everything they need to know in order to appreciate your application.

Imagine yourself as the reviewer. While you wouldn't want to be spoken to as though you were stupid, it is also true that you wouldn't mind being oriented by a clear statement of the basics at the opening of the project description. Therefore, in your writing, explain everything clearly and succinctly. It is encouraging to know that most reviewers do want to be on your side. I talked to a scholar who, in addition to being a frequent reviewer and the recipient of numerous prestigious grants, was employed by an agency as a scientific officer to watch the review process. (In this capacity, she worked for the agency, but on behalf of the candidates.) She said she had never seen reviewers who failed to take their job seriously and that the job of reviewers is to make sure that good research gets funded.

The Square Hole

If there is a *fundamental* disconnect between your project and the requirements of the granting agency, face it and deal with it up front rather than hoping you can bury it so well that the reviewers will not notice it. (If the problem is minor, it is probably best to overlook it. See sidebar entitled "When to Address the Gaps" in chapter 5.) The disconnect might involve what appears to be a change in career direction (all of your academic work to date has been in the field of astronomy, and now you are applying for funds for a psychology project), or the fact that you are applying for two small projects rather than one major project, or your inability to provide evidence of achievement in one of eight areas the application guidelines have asked you to address.

Grant-writing procrastination often results from the applicant's inability to deal with a central problem. You know what that problem is. You are convinced that the reviewers will see it, and you have no idea how to gloss it over. The procrastinating part of you is sure that no matter how well you disguise or embed the problem, it is going to be discovered and lead to your application being denied—so why bother completing it in the first place?

You must admit the problem clearly to yourself, and you must decide whether there is any point in continuing with the application. If necessary, ask for expert guidance—for example, from the granting agency itself. If there *is* still reason to continue, put the problem on the table and provide a thorough explanation as to why it should not eliminate your application from consideration. For example, you might explain how the psychology study arises naturally and logically from your research in astronomy, or show how two smaller projects will have greater impact than one major project on your overall research program, or provide evidence about how your strength in seven areas overshadows your shortcomings in the eighth.

If you face this problem—and all problems you encounter in applying for a grant—head on, everything will go more smoothly, from writing the submission to securing approval.

NOW THAT YOU HAVE LOOKED at your project in the larger picture and spent some time considering what it would be like to be someone who reviewed your application, you are ready to get down to the specifics.

☙ *A Note for Graduate Students*

WORKING WITH YOUR SUPERVISOR

With good reason, many students greatly admire their graduate supervisors, recognizing the extensive work those individuals are doing in research and teaching, quite aside from their administrative responsibilities. Some students, however, are so awed by their supervisors that they are reluctant to "bother" them.

Do not hesitate to solicit your supervisor's advice. By so, you are contributing to his or her scholarship as well as to your own. Training new researchers furthers the evolution of established academics as scholars and is a requirement for funding and advancement in many institutions. Teachers always learn from the experience of teaching.

- Think of the research you are developing with your supervisor as combining your different strengths—your supervisor has the balance and experience, and you have fresh perspectives and ideas.
- When applying for scholarships, make clear the connection between the supervisor's program and your application. Reviewers will look for evidence that actual mentorship is taking place. Make sure, too, that your supervisor is one of the writers of your letters of support.
- Ask for your supervisor's advice about putting together a good team to help you work through the application process, understanding that the people who help you with the description of your research plan and data analysis will be particularly important.
- Work closely with your supervisor in developing your scholarship or grant application. Keep your supervisor updated on your progress regularly—even if only by email. By keeping your supervisor involved, you will give him or her a greater stake in the outcome of your application—and it is

human nature to want to contribute to the success of initiatives in which we have a stake.

In general, even when your supervisor is extremely busy and distracted, you need to insist on spending time with him or her. It is wise to remind your supervisor occasionally about your genuine enthusiasm for the scholarly aspects of the projects you are working on together and to make intelligent observations and to ask relevant questions about the work and your field of study, rather than just conversing about daily routines. Accept your end of the responsibility for keeping the communication lines open.

TAKE CHARGE

You need to take responsibility for your funding application. Do not leave it to others to nag you to get going on it, or expect them to take you step by step through the application process. Even if they do so (which is unlikely), your lack of control over the process is going to show in the application itself. By the graduate-school level, you need to be thinking of other people, no matter how senior to you or more qualified than you, as your resources—not as substitute parents.

You care more than anyone else whether your funding application or scholarship application is outstanding. Your supervisor—while certainly interested in the outcome—has other things to think about, and so do your fellow students and colleagues. You are becoming a professional. Now is the time to take the lead role in the projects that affect your future. ▐

4

NOTES TOWARD THE TEXT

T here is still work you need to do before you begin writing the grant application. The next step is to focus your thoughts on the text component of the application—also known as the *narrative* or the *project description*. Here you will have a limited number of pages (depending on the agency, this may be as few as three or as many as fifteen) in which to convey a great deal of information concerning your project's history, context, potential impact, and other significant factors that can affect the outcome of your application.

Needless to say, how you present your ideas affects how your proposal is received. You need to communicate the value of the research project or program for which you are requesting funding, and you need to make it clear to the expert reviewers why you are the person (or team of people) who should receive the funding to do it—and why you should receive it now.

Your space is limited, so break down your information into manageable sections. Plan how much attention to devote to documenting your relevant experience, describing the project, explaining your project's position within your field of research, and so on. Some agencies indicate what portion of the text they wish to see devoted to specific subject areas, either by providing an outline of issues they want applicants to address or by structuring the application so that applicants are (for example) given two pages to describe their research background and five to describe the project. Funding agencies may also offer specific guidance regarding content and proportions in their brochures or on their websites.

Keep in mind that not all of the information you think the reviewers ought to have about your project will necessarily be requested in the agency's guidelines. Provide the information anyway, but decide how to fit it into the format the agency has requested. There is no point in including an extra page of text beyond the permitted length, no matter how critical you believe the information on that extra page to be, because it is likely that the reviewers will not see it. Even when you have a designated outline, however, you can take charge of your application. It is up to you to decide how to organize the information and how to communicate it within the allocated space.

What You Want to Tell Them

At the preliminary planning stage, you may find it useful to open a separate document file on your computer or a page in a notebook for each of the components of the project description. Examples are:

- Context/Setting
- Rationale
- Literature Review
- Methodology
- Collaborators
- Training of Others
- Outcomes
- Research Environment
- Personal Background/Experience
- Previous Grants
- Dissemination

You can add notes to these files as thoughts occur to you, create new files if you think of additional areas you want to cover, and even begin to combine and synthesize the material within the files—all in advance of the actual writing.

Here are some areas that you may find it valuable to address in your application. The specific requirements in the funding guidelines and the familiarity of the selection committee with your area of research will determine the relevance of each of these areas for a particular application.

- *Background information* that may be necessary for reviewers to understand your project, including the nature of your specific area of research, and how it fits into your discipline. Depending on your perception of your review panel's knowledge level (based on your research about its members), you might need to explain the basics (e.g., what medical genetics is and how it fits into the wider field of biomedical research) or only provide specific information (such as how techniques involving fluorescent in situ hybridization contribute to cytogenetics).
- *The important issue* your project will address and the importance of the research to scholarly investigation in your field (e.g., why your findings regarding the use of egg tempera in post-Byzantine art will contribute substantially to the ongoing debate about artists' choices of materials).
- *What scholars know already* about the issue you are studying and how your work can be seen as innovative—and timely—in your field.
- *How your study will be conducted* and how outcomes will be measured.
- *With whom you are working* on this investigation and why you are working with these particular individuals/team members. You may also describe, if appropriate, the features of your particular university or research institution that make it an ideal place for you to carry out your work.
- *Opportunities you will provide* during the course of your research to undergraduate and/or graduate students, postdoctoral fellows, and/or other new researchers in order to advance their training and knowledge.

- *Why you are a good person* to receive funding. Describe your relevant background and other pertinent achievements, and how the current research fits into your ongoing career.
- *What you have achieved* with previous research funding.
- *How you plan to report* on and disseminate your findings.

Planning the Structure

Lists such as the one above, plus the application form, the funding-agency guidelines, and the other resources you are able to access, will help you organize the points you must address in your proposal's text in order to meet the agency's criteria. These components may also help you develop a list of other topics to include that will strengthen your position with the reviewers. Your primary goal when you start writing your project description is to make it clear to those reviewing your application that you are addressing all of the requirements the agency has set out. Within that framework you still have some flexibility and therefore some control over the impression your proposal makes.

Location can be as important as content when it comes to presenting information. All of us have read papers or articles in which the authors failed to mention a salient detail until it was too late to influence the reader's first reactions. (Consider, for example, an application that explains that prolonged bouts of hiccups can lead to life-threatening depressions only *after* a reviewer has read enough to throw down the papers, ask what sort of organization would give someone $400,000 to study folk remedies for hiccups, and go off to eat dinner.)

Planning ahead can ensure the most effective order of presentation for your material, and it can also prevent repetition—resulting in the waste of precious square inches of application space. If you have conducted previous research into the effectiveness of the startle response in stopping hiccups in chimpanzees, you must decide whether it is more effective to include this information in the "project description" or the "background experience" section. With limited space, there is certainly no point in including it twice.

On Logic

The study of logic is associated with the fields of philosophy and mathematics and is applicable in a range of other settings as well. Logic is the process of developing solid conclusions from sound principles.

Basing conclusions on reliable principles or structures is an essential component of all scientific investigation, and of all forms of argument and persuasion based on intellect. Many of us were taught in high school that if you want to test a theory or to extend it by means of an argument, the propositions or statements that make up the underlying hypothesis must be sound. People who are writing research hypotheses for grant proposals are familiar with how to develop and explain assumptions, as well as with identifying variables and building hypotheses. You do not want to set out to prove theories that are already accepted principles or to attempt to prove the unprovable.

The benefits of logical discourse are not, of course, restricted to academic settings. Most television viewers appreciate the role of logical thinking in the resolution of made-for-television crimes, and many phone users have experienced the effects of a lack of logic when attempting to compare long-distance rates.

The media frequently draw erroneous conclusions from sound science. All of us cringe on behalf of investigators when we see this happen. (A respected publication once announced, "Research shows that God answers prayers," in a headline intended to attract attention to an article about a study that had found a slight positive correlation between prayer and desired outcome.)

Fallacious arguments make their way into grant proposals, too—even from senior scholars. The fault often lies in the writing of the applications, and the errors are not reflected in the research plans

Logic: A Very Short Introduction, by Graham Priest, *A Rulebook for Arguments,* by Anthony Weston, and *The Art of Thinking: A Guide to Critical and Creative Thought,* by Vincent Ryan Ruggiero, all provide useful overviews of logic and its use in argument. (See the annotated bibliography for additional information on these and other resources.)

Graham Priest provides a basic introduction to the complex subject of logic. He explains the host of technical terms associated with this branch of philosophy in language the lay reader can understand, provides a brief history of the evolution of logical thinking from the time of Plato to today, and challenges the reader with a range of brain-twisting examples—all in only 128 pages.

Anthony Weston's book is brief, too. Within only 87 pages, he manages to list approximately thirty rules he considers essential to the development of valid arguments, and to explain and provide examples of each rule. Weston rounds out his book with definitions of common labels used to identify thinking errors in rhetoric (e.g., "straw man," "begging the question," and "ad hominem arguments"), a three-part guide to the development of a sound written argument, and suggestions for further reading on related topics.

Based on his convictions that good thinkers are made, not born, and that the habits of good thinking can be taught and learned, Vincent Ryan Ruggiero has addressed the subject of thinking critically and creatively in his interesting book. *The Art of Thinking* is divided into four sections ("Be Aware," "Be Creative," "Be Critical," and "Communicate Your Ideas"), each of which offers a range of topics and examples that assist in the development of clear and logical reading and writing skills. The book is perhaps more appropriate for students than for established scholars, but its host of tips and series of increasingly complex mental exercises will appeal to most academic readers. In a four-page appendix, Ruggiero summarizes the principles of formal logic.

themselves. For example, even when the proposed work is built on solid supporting evidence, applicants may neglect to draw a clear line from A to B to C for the benefit of reviewers. This omission may be due in part to the fact that being exposed to an area of research can limit our ability to see the forest for the trees, but it may also be due to a failure to consider the principles of logic.

Consider these statements: "A person has served time in prison.

This person must therefore have committed a crime." This simple example of illogical thinking is based on the faulty assumption that all people who are found guilty of crimes and sentenced to jail are, in fact, guilty. The logical counterpart of this example is, "A person has served time in prison. This person must therefore have been found guilty of committing a crime." (The second sentence is technically known as a "valid inference.")

Logic—which includes such components as deductive reasoning, recognizing fallacies, and syllogisms, and the use of premises, inferences and conclusions—is a fascinating field of study and may be undertaken in passing or in depth. Many overviews of the subject are available online or in print, on topics that range from the use of logic in scientific and mathematical study and computer contexts to its use in communication. (See the sidebar "A Logical Place to Start" for the titles of books that provide an introduction to the field of logic.) Resources tailored to the building of sound argument (as in debating or speech writing) or other forms of intellectual persuasion (some forms of marketing) are also potentially valuable in writing research-grant proposals, as well as in dozens of other contexts.

No matter how evident it may seem to you that your project is of value, you still need to develop a strong and logical case to convince a granting agency to support it. Review panels are eager to fund good projects, but they are made up of experts for a reason: experts are able to find flaws. If there is a gap in logic in your presentation, you can be sure that someone on the panel is going to find it and point it out.

Connecting Other Dots

In addition to developing your proposal so that it builds logically from A to B to C, you also need to keep in mind the target audience, and draw a strong connection between audience and project. No explanation of your proposed work—no matter how solid and finely crafted—can be suitable for every situation, because every funding agency has different interests and goals.

One researcher I spoke with studies the psychological needs of children with specific health disorders. Her work might be eligible for funding from a variety of agencies—one that supported the work of pediatric psychologists, for example, or one supporting educators, or one devoted to funding health specialists. She would be well advised to tailor a significant portion of her project description to emphasize the specific agency's area of interest. In the case of research-support proposals, one size does not fit all.

Especially in applying to a cross-disciplinary program, or to a program for which your area of study is not an obvious match due to some novel connection you have made between two different fields of study, you need far more than a tagline to remind the reviewers why your project is appropriate for their consideration. Whenever you are aware that the review committee or a segment of it brings a certain perspective to the table, it is critical to keep that perspective in mind throughout the application-writing process. Reviewers will not make the connection between your work and their funding mandate or area of knowledge for you. You need to make the connection *for them*.

The Whole Package

As you develop your notes toward beginning to write your application, always keep an eye on the big picture. The application form and guidelines from the funding agency, plus additional points you choose to emphasize in your proposal, will help you select and shape the supporting materials to include in the submission package. Decisions about all of the following supporting materials can be made with a view to strengthening your application:

- which published articles and unpublished papers to send (where applicable)
- which references to cite

- whom you should invite to write letters of support for you
- points to suggest that your letter writers include in their letters

Starting your application process well in advance of the deadline gives you an opportunity to compile a substantive, strong application that includes supporting materials carefully selected to enhance specific aspects of your funding proposal.

NOW YOU HAVE ASSEMBLED all the data and other information you need in order to sit down and write the application. You are clear about the work you want to undertake, you know exactly how it fits with the agency's mandate, and you feel utterly confident about your ability to carry out the project in a way that will meet or exceed all agency expectations—and possibly even your own. Now you are ready—and you should be eager—to get this application done.

✒ *A Note for Graduate Students*

CREATING A STRONG FUNDING APPLICATION

The purpose of your funding application is to prove that you can do what you say you can do. You need to be impressive without sounding overly confident. (You are still a graduate student after all, and as you have probably noticed, no matter what you have achieved or how much respect you deserve, no one will allow you to become too self-important just yet.) But don't be modest, either. You need to show your ambition and your genuine interest in your subject.

The following tips may be of use in developing an effective graduate-level funding application.

- Cast a wide net over your past experience before you start writing so that you are able to show reviewers why you are an outstanding candidate. Even though your previous research experience, related professional background, and list of publications are limited at this stage, you can mention course work that has had a particular relevance, related undergraduate experiences and other achievements that may (even peripherally) be connected to your present studies (such as extracurricular and volunteer work), and skills you have acquired in full-time or part-time employment before or during graduate school.

- Applicants in doctoral programs should always show a clear connection between the work they did in their master's programs and what they are doing now. If it appears that you have changed directions in your program of study, show the reviewers the line of thought that took you from where you were to where you are. Was there something in your master's program that caught your attention and interest, leading you toward a new area of work? If so, tell the reader what it was. When you make such connections clear, you contribute to the perception of yourself as a centered, cohesive kind of individual.

- Explain why you are working with a specific supervisor and why you have chosen to do your graduate studies at a specific university. On some scholarship applications, there is a space that allows for this kind of explanation. I have seen students leave it blank because they felt there was no need to explain. Always take advantage of blank spaces if you can. It *is* worthwhile to point out the strengths of your supervisor and your university. Doing so reflects well on you. It makes you sound like a team player, which is beneficial to you not only with those reviewing applications at the agency level but also with the people from your university or college who will see this application, too.

- In addition to your supervisor, talk to the staff and consultants in your graduate studies office for tips on applying. These people have seen the worst and the best from many disciplines and can provide you with useful advice.

- Talk to students who have been successful with similar scholarship applications in the past. Ask to see their successful applications. Carefully consider what they have done and what lessons you can apply to your own application.

- When asking for letters of reference, you may wish to remind your referees of the significance of what you are applying for and to explain that you appreciate that the letters they write are going to make a major difference to how your application is received by the reviewers. Your goal is to let the referees know that, if they do not feel that they are able to write a thorough and enthusiastic letter of support for you, you would like to be given the opportunity to ask someone else. ▌

5

UN-CURB YOUR
ENTHUSIASM

· ·

Think about standing in the grocery store trying to decide between two products on the shelf: both have the same purpose, but one is more expensive than the other. (This is a product you are going use to clean your bathtub, so it's not like you are worried about flavor.) The more expensive product has a well-known brand name, and its packaging is familiar and appealing (maybe even "sexy"!); the packaging of the other is boring, reflecting its lower price, and you have never heard of the manufacturer. You check the list of ingredients, and they are the same. Both packages contain the same amount of product. The contents even *look* the same—same color and consistency as far as you can tell.

If you are like most people, despite all of the evidence right before your eyes, you are still nervous about buying the cheaper product. Why? Well, in all likelihood the marketing of the more expensive product has convinced you that it is somehow better. You have seen ads for it in magazines and on television, and a part of your brain is telling you that because its name is familiar and its packaging is more attractive, it is somehow safer or superior to the other product in a way that you cannot even put your finger on.

You are an intelligent and highly educated individual. You have been trained to think, to evaluate, to draw logical conclusions from available data. But in certain situations, your thinking is not always rational—as you are reminded when you pick the brand-name product off the shelf and place it in your cart.

Clearly, attracting interest in a bathroom cleanser is quite a different undertaking from attracting interest in a research project, but when it comes to getting the message across, some of the same principles apply. We are all susceptible to persuasive presentation. Not only do you need to construct a strong and well-organized argument to "sell" your idea to reviewers, you need to make your argument appeal to them on an emotional level by writing in a captivating way.

You need to help your reviewers buy into what you are doing. You need to get them on your side. Show them that this idea of yours is novel, that it is an idea whose time has come. You do that by sharing your enthusiasm.

Where Is Your Passion?

By the time most people sit down to write a funding application for any given research project, they have been working with much of the same material for several years. If this is true of you, then you have probably already presented the work a number of times—at conferences, in articles, in research groups, in applications to other granting agencies. You know how to go about assembling the facts and putting them down on paper. Your list of publications, supporting documentation, and names of potential outside experts are all in order. You see this current application as one in a long list of administrative hurdles you need to clear so you can do your research.

I am falling asleep just imagining the state of mind you must be in.

That state of mind (bored, resigned, skeptical about the outcome, weary, all of the above—am I getting close?) is going to be reflected in your application unless you take steps to make sure that it is not. States of mind are contagious, as you know well if you have ever listened to a conference presenter delivering a talk in a monotonic drone. If your project description is dull and pedestrian, the reviewers are going to feel that—and they will be alienated. Why should they care about such boring research? Why should this undertaking matter to them, when it is obviously not of much interest even to the researcher? When requests for research support greatly exceed the funds available, why should reviewers feel anything but relief at being able to put aside one application because it is not remarkable in any way?

I am not suggesting that you submit your application in a neon folder embedded with computer chips that play a tune when the folder is opened or cause little colored lights to blink all over the bibliography—or that you inject superlatives (or expletives) throughout the text in order to attract attention. I am simply encouraging you to recall what got you into this field of study in the first place and to let the undercurrent of excitement that drew you to your particular area of investigation come through in your writing of—and in your approach to your writing of—your funding proposal. Like boredom, enthusiasm is contagious.

I worked on a project a few years ago with an individual at Carleton University in Ottawa who is head of the Procrastination Research Institute. Now there is a subject that could be considered a downer if ever there was one, especially in academic settings. Procrastination has prevented tens of thousands of students from completing their degrees, prevented scores of academics from attracting the promotions they might otherwise deserve, and induced feelings of anguish and self-loathing in millions of people around the world. Yet there was no mistaking Tim Pychyl's enthusiasm for his chosen area of research—you heard it in his voice when you talked to him, and it was reflected in his writing on the subject. You could feel it even when you were looking at his website. His enthusiasm made you feel enthusiastic about the subject, too. (The URL for Pychyl's work is included in the resource list, but do not get involved in it now and forget about your application. Keep your finger in this page! Come back!)

Show It, Don't Tell It

"Show, don't tell" is a fundamental principle of creative writing, and it also has a role to play in making your research-funding application attractive to reviewers. You do not generate interest in your work by telling people that your work is interesting. You do not convince reviewers that you have the potential to alter life by telling them your results will be life-altering. You do not persuade anyone that you are the best researcher in your field by saying that you are the best researcher in the field. In most cases, the "I am great because I say I am" approach will get your application thrown right out the door.

While avoiding the use of such words as *greatest, genius,* and *mind-boggling* in the application itself, you can profitably keep such epithets front and center in your mind while you are writing. If you believe in your own work, your confidence will be obvious in your description of it. If you are enthusiastic about your work, your enthusiasm will show in your presentation. You do not need to say "I am enthusiastic," but your application needs to radiate your energy, confidence, and optimism.

Overcome the Mental Blocks

What mental blocks are causing you to hide your light under a barrel?

You may have come to the conclusion through various experiences that your area of study is inherently boring. ("Just ask those people I met at the baseball game last weekend," you're thinking. "*They* didn't want to hear about my work.") Before you go any further you need to recognize the basic flaw in this reasoning. *Nothing is inherently boring.* It is all a matter of presentation—the "spin," to use the marketing jargon. Even dull subjects can be described in a way that makes them intriguing to the reader, without stretching the truth at all. It is up to *you* to find the *unboring* way to present your work.

I continue to meet academics who have no idea how interesting their research is to other people—to lay people as well as to researchers in their own and other disciplines. (Like everyone else, I also meet academics with the opposite problem: they never *stop* talking about their work. Here, too, the problems are perception and presentation.) If anyone should know in what ways your research is interesting, it is you. You must have been attracted to your area of research and scholarly endeavor by something at some point—or what are you doing with your life? (If you are not certain what you are doing with your life, please note that this question goes beyond the issues I am addressing in this book. You probably do not have time to consider it in any great depth at the moment anyway, so I recommend that you stop thinking about it. Think instead about something that *does* interest you—such as the new computer program you will be able to justify purchasing if your application is successful.)

Even if you don't think your work is boring, maybe you doubt that you are qualified to be doing what you are doing. This is a common feeling (much as we would like to hide it from our colleagues). Many people are kept awake at night by visions of Mensa-eligible researchers who are at this minute completing applications for the very funding that the insomniacs long to have. Lack of self-confidence is common among intelligent people—early in their careers, of course, but also at midcareer or even later when they suddenly take on a larger challenge than they have faced before or when they enter a new field. It is as if their brain capacities allow them not only to do what they are doing to the best of their abilities but also simultaneously to stand outside themselves and become their own worst critics.

The issue of self-confidence is larger than what this volume is intended to address. However, much can be done to overcome feelings of inadequacy with appropriate self-talk. For example, if you are overly focused on the fact that at this point in your career you are not yet making prize-winning contributions in your field, then try to think instead of how many miles you would need to go before you could find a single person (excluding any other members of your own research group, of course) who knows as much as you do about your particular area of specialty. Would it be two hundred miles? Five hundred? A thousand?

Are you failing to give yourself proper credit? Many academics grow so used to discussing discipline-specific knowledge with their colleagues on a daily basis that they lose track of how much they actually know. They fail to think about how many other academics their work has affected, and in what ways. You have no doubt influenced not only your current and former students but also people who have read about your work, and others you have met at national and international meetings or talked to via e-mail. Many academics have not considered how their area of research has moved forward in the past twenty years, or how cross-disciplinary their work has become, or how much knowledge they have acquired while these changes were taking place.

Think about your next-door neighbors. What could you tell them about the things you have accomplished since your academic life began—and how enthused you are about the progress you have made? What words would be especially useful in explaining what intrigues you about your area of research? If your work is particularly technical, what analogies could you use to make it easier to understand?

The Right Frame of Mind

How do you progress from boredom to enthusiasm? How do you rearrange your mind so that your passion shines straight through your writing and lights up the minds of your reviewers? Exactly the same way I drew myself away from reading the newspaper this morning and got to work on writing this chapter: by deliberately changing my mind. I focused on the reasons why I wanted to get a draft of this chapter done today and visualized how I would feel

In the grant-writing workshops I run, I ask participants from different disciplines, or at least from different subdisciplines—preferably people they have never spoken with before—to form groups of three or four. I give participants ten minutes to write a "pitch." (In this context, *pitch* may be thought of as a term taken from marketing, scriptwriting, or baseball—it contains elements of all three.) They need to explain the project, put it in context, give evidence as to why it is worthy of funding, and show why they are ideally positioned to carry out this work. Each individual presents his or her pitch to the group, and the other group members are then required to ask the kinds of questions that a reviewer might ask about the project or the program.

Such small-group exercises may be offered in departmental research-study groups or in other academic settings, too. If necessary you can attain almost the same result independently with a slightly different exercise. Set yourself the task of creating a coherent and interesting three-minute response that you can use the next time you are at a party and a stranger asks you what you do for a living, or asks you to describe your area of research. Create a summary that is clear and interesting—one that you can actually use in the future to make people want to hear more, rather than less, about what you do. No apologies are necessary. Just give them the basic facts about what makes your work so fascinating.

when the chapter was finished—and, even better, how I would feel when the book was in print.

Before you start writing your funding proposal, you need to take a few minutes to think about such questions as:

- What got you interested in this area of research in the first place?
- How did you *feel* when you were first interested? Why?
- What is the best part of the work you are undertaking now? How does *that* make you *feel*?
- What is the positive outcome you are anticipating after all the hard work is done? How would you *feel* if you got this grant, for example?
- How would you *feel* if you got an e-mail from one of your peers

who had seen your proposal as a member of the review panel and wanted more information about your work?

Imagine yourself after this grant has come in, working on your project. Imagine submitting your report on the grant's successful completion. Imagine an outcome that is so successful that you are nominated for a prize.

By asking yourself questions and focusing on your emotional responses to them (thus, the *feelings*), you put yourself into the state of mind that you need to be in when you write your proposal—and if you *feel* it, that state of mind will come through in your writing. Show your reviewers your enthusiasm for your work and help them begin to feel personally connected to the work you are doing. Get them on your side. By the time they are finished reading your proposal, *they* should be *feeling* that they cannot wait to see the outcome of the work they are about to recommend for funding.

In short, each time before you start to write, close your eyes for a few minutes and allow yourself to adopt the mood you want to pass on to your readers.

Accentuate the Positive

Unfortunately, our negative thoughts are often reflected in what we write. Most of us are easily able to find the flaws in our past performance, despairing over the caliber of the journals we have published in, the low prestige of our undergraduate institution, or perhaps events in our personal lives that have delayed our academic advancement. Specific negative thoughts can also affect how we write about our work.

- You spend your time thinking about the three-year drought when you did not publish anything.
- You focus on what you know about the politics of the journal editorial board you sit on.
- You wonder why you have been invited to give only one significant presentation so far in your career.

Obviously, there are times when we wish things had gone differently for us, and from those experiences the best we can do is learn from our mistakes and try not to dwell on them.

For the negative thoughts listed above, consider that there are other ways to look at them.

- There were many years when you did publish, and many of your publications are of the highest quality.
- Sitting on that journal editorial board is giving you a strong credential.
- The invitation to present was earned; it was *not* just a lucky break.

Academics need to be accurate in everything they report about their work and their track records—that goes without saying. Knowledge in all fields is advanced by building on the facts as we know them. Academic careers must be built on solid achievement. If somebody congratulates you on having an article published in a journal, you don't need to say it was rejected by a dozen other journals or that you wish it had been published elsewhere. That other person complimented you. Both you and that person will be a lot happier if you just say, "Thank you."

In the same way, you need to accentuate the positive in your application and avoid focusing on the negative. (Within reason—see "When to Address the Gaps.") Some people have more trouble doing this than others. In some parts of the world (and those "parts" are frequently defined by gender, ethnicity, socioeconomic status, and other variables as well as by geography), it is not considered "polite" to blow one's own horn. Those of us who have been raised in communities where displaying "pride" is sinful or is tantamount to inviting bad luck often come to the workplace with a reluctance to highlight our achievements. But a competition for research funding is no place for modesty. It is no place for apologies, self-negativity, or superstition. (Nor is it the place to feel awkward about "asking for money"—as many people naturally do. You are not asking for a

Whether or not to address an obvious inconsistency in your track record is largely a matter of common sense. Keep in mind that reviewers, pressed for time, are not likely to read your CV word for word. They are going to rely primarily on your project description, letters of support, and other directly relevant documents, and to refer to the CV only in passing for elaboration or clarification, if at all. There is probably no point in explaining career interruptions or program delays unless you have been specifically requested to do so. Is it absolutely necessary to raise the matter of the one-year gap between the completion of your master's program and the commencement of your doctorate if you would really rather not talk about it? Must you point out that you were not promoted from assistant to associate professor quite as quickly as most of your colleagues, and then explain why? If a detail has little impact on your current work and is already set out somewhere in your CV should anyone care to look, ask yourself whether the reviewers would even notice or care about it if you did not point it out to them.

If, on the other hand, you took time off to fly to the moon or have a baby and you feel it is useful to mention that, then do. And if the gap or non sequitur *is* likely to have an impact on your current work—if, for example, you changed specialties from gynecology to oncology, or if half of your published papers are in history journals and the other half in medical journals—you are well advised to address those kinds of incongruities in a note.

What you are doing in the latter case is to *manage* the impression you are making. And managing the impression is the essence of effective self-promotion.

handout. If you get this funding, you will have earned it, and you will also pay for it, in the work you do after you receive the grant.)

Failing to put your strengths and your achievements in the best possible light is like shooting yourself in the foot; you won't get far that way. Keep in mind, too, that if you appear hesitant about your qualifications, reviewers may doubt your ability to carry out the project.

Some people need outside help to see their own negative or timid thinking. If you suspect that you suffer from this problem, get someone who is not shy to read your application with a view to finding and eliminating hesitancy and negativity. You may even need to get that person to help you rewrite the material so that it is stronger and more effective—particularly those sections that deal with your competence to do the work, lead the project, accomplish the mission.

You do not need to brag, lie, or exaggerate. But you do need to be self-confident and positive. Unless your fellow applicants are all utterly unqualified for the funds you are seeking, adopting a heads-up, shoulders-back posture will be essential to your success.

❧ *A Note for Graduate Students*

DEALING WITH CRITICISM

You will probably need to apply more than once before you are successful with a scholarship or graduate-project funding application. The ability to cope with criticism and make constructive use of it can help to make these applications part of the learning process rather than exercises in frustration. Listen to your professors and your supervisor, and pay close attention to any feedback on your application that you receive from the staff in your institution's graduate studies and/or research offices. Make note of all constructive criticism you receive during this process, and use the suggestions that you find to be of value.

Students at the graduate level can be immobilized by concerns over the increased levels of competition they are encountering compared with their undergraduate experiences. Keep in mind that you are one of the graduate students, too, and you got here the same way all the others did. You are all starting out on your careers. There is no point in trying to compensate for what you may *think* you lack: just state what you have done and leave it at that. Don't explain. Don't justify. You are what you are. On the application, it is better to write "not applicable" (n/a) than to write "I don't have any experience in this area because ... "

A mistake some students make when developing a project

description is to attempt to address every single point of criticism their project has ever received, thereby deflecting criticisms preemptively one by one. This creates tangents that interrupt the flow of the writing. Keep in mind that every writer who sees your application is going to have questions, and you cannot anticipate them all. Take an offensive rather than defensive approach. Focus on getting the important points across to readers in a smooth, clear comprehensive manner, as described elsewhere in this book. Distract reviewers from their own questions with the strength of your proposal. ▌▐

6

THE BUDGET
Core Strength

....

The budget is the "main act" of your funding application. The other elements of your proposal describe the context and purpose of your project, but the ultimate goal of the grant-application process—getting money to do your project—is fundamentally expressed in dollars and cents (or in euros, pounds, etc.). It is also on the basis of those precise and concrete units of currency that you will need to submit your final report. The budget is not a support document to be tacked on to your application at the last moment; it is essential to the package, and its accuracy and completeness are critical to the outcome of your application.

Funding agencies and review panels scrutinize your budget, which to them is not merely a statement of the anticipated costs related to your research project but is an indication of the validity of the plan you have created to carry out your work, the practicality of your approach, and your capacity to bring the project to a business-like conclusion. The budget and the notes contained in the budget-justification document demonstrate to the reviewers your grasp of the project and your ability to carry out your plan.

In a well-developed funding proposal, budget items reflect and reinforce every aspect of every step set out in the project description. Throughout the application-development process, therefore, consider the budget to be the framework that supports the entire structure.

Understand the Agency's Budgetary Guidelines

You need to know exactly what expenses the agency will fund and in what terms it describes each item. Some smaller funding agencies will not contribute at all to what are generally called "indirect," "overhead," or "facilities and administrative" (F&A) costs. These are the ongoing costs, probably including your own salary, which your home institution pays whether or not you get the grant. For agencies that do subsidize indirect costs, as is the case with most government-supported funding sources, each one has its own formulae for determining the amount of the contribution.

Definitions of allowable direct costs can vary by agency, as well. One agency may consider consultants to be "personnel," whereas others will want salaried staff to be listed separately from individuals to whom fees are paid. By "equipment," some agencies mean only capital expenditures over a certain dollar value; others define the term more broadly. Do research before you start. If you request funding for an expense that is not allowed by the agency, or enter the cost of a microscope under "capital equipment" when it should have been listed under "other equipment," you may slow down or halt the processing of your application.

Find out if the agency has any requirements for cost sharing (which normally means that the home institution agrees to contribute a portion of the cost of the project, at least by way of "in-kind" support) or for matching funding (where an actual commitment of dollars from other sources may be required). If you need to show evidence that your home institution agrees to the conditions regarding in-kind or matching income, allow time to obtain the necessary documents.

If you are asked to submit a project budget (rather than a list of expenses for which you are requesting agency funding), you must include all the costs that will be incurred in the successful completion of your project, including those that are not part of your request to the agency. Budgets must be comprehensive: you cannot omit an expense simply because it does not fall within an agency's guidelines. If a specific instrument is required to test the samples you collect, you must include the cost of purchasing or using that instrument in the budget. Show clearly how you plan to pay for any expenditure in the budget that will not be covered by the grant.

Budgets must also balance: all expenses must be offset by income. If the total cost of your project exceeds the amount you hope to receive from the funding agency, you must indicate the source of the balance of the income.

Finally, investigate the typical amount of grants that have been awarded to projects such as yours by the agency in recent years. Be sure that you are able to conduct the research described in your application within the agency's typical funding range.

Budget Items

Even if it is not a requirement, as it is at several universities and colleges, it is worthwhile to work closely with the grants officers and development officers at your home institution to create a budget that is comprehensive and meets all institutional guidelines. The table on pages 72 and 73 is provided primarily as an aid to readers who may not have access to this kind of administrative support. It can also be used as a preliminary guide while you are drafting the headings you will use in your budget.

When calculating costs, use the relevant "metric" or guideline (for example, for personnel hours or mileage rates) established by the funding agency or by your home institution.

Like all of your other documents, the budget should be as clear and easy as possible for the reviewers to read. Even if the agency does not require it, break down projects that cover extended time periods into funding segments or modules (Year 1, Year 2, etc.) to make the information even easier for readers to assimilate. To enhance the clarity of the proposal's structure, some candidates include timelines in their narratives that show the unfolding of the different sections of the research project by funding period, and some candidates even place the specific project in the context of a wider research program where that is appropriate or useful. Once completed, the budget you have created can serve as a template for applications you make to various agencies for years to come. There will be slight modifications depending on the agency to which you are applying and the particular project, but in the course of your career, you are likely to find that many of the costs recur in your various research projects. You will need to check each item for each application to make sure that it is still relevant and is still eligible for support, and that costs for particular supplies or services have not changed significantly. It is also worthwhile to take apart your "typical" budget from time to time, or even to rebuild it from scratch, to make sure that it has not become outdated, disorganized, and meaningless.

If you are submitting a revised funding application, reread the guidelines carefully to find out whether the agency has changed its rules since the last time you applied.

Budget Justification

Find out how many pages you are permitted for the "budget justification"—the notes you include to justify all but the most obvious budget entries. By means of this narrative, also known as the "budget narrative," you make sure that each budget item is clearly connected to the proposal. (For example, if the work is to be carried out by two investigators, explain the different responsibilities each of them will have. These responsibilities should in turn relate directly to the investigator biographies, which will be included in a separate attachment.) The budget justification is also the place to clarify the bases on which you derived each budget amount. (For example, explain when and on what basis you obtained your estimates for the cost of accommodations in the field.) Finally, the budget justification is where you explain any items not specifically tied to the

Typical expenditures listed in grant applications

Category	Item	To Consider
Personnel/employees • investigators • project administrators • research assistants • trainees/students • technical support • subcontractors • replacement personnel	• salaries/wages • benefits • insurance	• In budget justification, note role, duties, investment of time/effort required for each individual/position • If specific individuals will be needed for only specific periods of time during the project, the budget should reflect that • Include recruitment costs where applicable
Outside consultants	• fees	• Obtain quotes in writing where appropriate
Travel • domestic • foreign	• air, train, bus, taxi • other public transport • rental of vehicles • food • accommodation • insurance	• Clarify agency definition of "domestic" and "foreign" • Itemize (do not guess: obtain quotes) • Use regular rather than discounted fares • Use established per-diem rates for food and vehicle-mileage rates where available
Supplies	All expenses directly connected to the project that will be incurred in the laboratory, the field, the office—e.g., lab supplies, computer disks, pens, paper, notebooks.	• Itemize • Do not go overboard, but do not underestimate either • Use past lists of expenditures by you or other researchers to develop estimates and avoid omissions
Resources	• reference books • conferences and workshops • consultations • software	• Must relate to project • Use budget justification section where needed
Equipment/capital costs	• computers • cameras • microscopes	• Make sure that you are familiar with the agency's guidelines for the purchase of capital equipment • Justify each item

	• other equipment and/or apparatus related to the research but useful beyond the research period; normally costing more than a specified amount	• Provide specific estimates • Include costs for maintenance, insurance, installation, depreciation where applicable • Share costs where possible
Services	• media specialists • computer support • data analysis/processing • caregivers for animals	• Charge only for time required • Include recruitment costs if necessary • May be distinct item from consultants' fees or may be amalgamated
Rental/lease of space Renovations of space		• Itemize • Justify
Communications	• telephone • postage, couriers • conference calls • teleconferencing • Internet costs during fieldwork • translation services	• Take care not to duplicate expenses in this category with those covered under "indirect costs"
Dissemination and/or commercialization	• preparing manuscripts, e.g. editing costs, indexing • publishing costs	
Indirect costs (overhead, facilities/administrative costs)	Includes ongoing costs of office space, laboratories, library services, other administrative costs	• Get advice from your research department regarding these costs, which the agency may assign on a formula basis • Where agencies do not fund indirect costs, special dispensation in writing from your institution may be required before a funding application can be submitted
Other	• Inflation • Taxes	Fees associated with belonging to research consortia may be included here if not elsewhere

Note: This table does not include the kinds of living expenses that would be required by individuals applying to carry out artistic projects or those incurred in the administration and execution of large capital projects by scientific consortia, art galleries, museums, and so forth. See specific agencies for criteria in relation to these and all funding programs.

proposal. (For example, point out that the roll of bubble wrap listed under Supplies is required to protect equipment for transport to the field.)

Agencies provide a format for the budget narrative. Normally, it resembles a page of endnotes.

Assessing Your Budget

While different agencies have different requirements for evaluating a budget, all agencies will consider such questions as the following:

- Is the budget thorough and reasonable? Does it show a genuine knowledge of what needs to be done to accomplish the goal of the project? Does it reflect current costs for materials and labor? (It is counterproductive to shave costs in the hope that if you ask for less you will stand a better chance of being funded: not only will you run the risk of appearing to the agency to be a poor cost estimator, you will also run out of money before the project is finished.)
- Notwithstanding the previous point, does the budget seem excessive?
- Does the budget reflect a realistic view of how long it will take to conduct the study and analyze and write up the results?
- Does the budget include money to pay consultants in areas where the research team lacks expertise? Does it include *enough* money for those consultants? Conversely, are such services available for less? (Do not merely guess at fees for outside expertise—or any other costs of which you are not sure. Obtain estimates so that, even if they are not included in the proposal itself, they can be made available on request to the funding agency.)
- Does the budget overlook anything or make any assumptions that may not translate into reality (e.g., that the price of gas will remain the same for three consecutive years)?

- Is the budget going to look questionable to third-party reviewers who may be looking over the shoulders of the panel members? (For example, does the budget justification demonstrate convincingly why you must conduct your research midwinter in the Caribbean rather than in your home city six months later?)

Budgets can be much more revealing than prose descriptions. The budget can show when researchers are biting off more than they can chew, when their projects are too narrow to be useful, and when omissions imperil the validity of their studies. If you are not a financial wizard, get someone who is adept at reading budgets to help you develop yours—or at least to review it prior to submission.

When to Create the Budget

Almost the first step you should take in the writing of a research proposal is to start the document in which you will generate your budget—often a spreadsheet, or a worksheet provided by the agency. As you have been doing in your planning for the text, you can "rough in" headings right at the beginning—adding to, refining, and combining them as you go along.

At the outset it is important only to set up categories and make notes under them. Resist the urge to get a finalized budget out of the way before you start the text; doing so is likely to be a waste of time. You will find yourself adding to the budget and even modifying its structure as you work through the rest of the application. If it is done properly, your budget and the accompanying narrative will not be ready for final review and formatting until everything else is finished—but when it is, you will be able to submit it with absolute confidence.

7

GET IT DOWN
The First Draft

....

To those who have just joined us: Welcome. No doubt you saw the words "The First Draft" in the table of contents and decided that chapter 7 was the place to start. You are probably wondering why I took six chapters to get down to the brass tacks.

I hate to break it to you new arrivals, but the readers who followed the suggestions in the first six chapters have done almost all of their work already. The hardest part of writing a grant application (or of writing anything) is the part that comes before you actually sit down to do it—the thinking, the planning, the note making, the prioritizing, the gathering or compiling or soliciting of support documents, and so on. After doing all that groundwork, by the time you get to the actual writing of the application you are on your way from third base to home plate.

However, since we are all human and therefore have all done things at the last minute, and since those who missed the first six chapters this time may find occasion to read them before their next application deadline, I do not intend to antagonize the tardy by omitting key points or making snarky references to how much better off you would be if you had followed a suggestion I made in chapter 2—and done it two months ago.

I do recommend going back to chapter 6, "The Budget: Core

Strength," and reading that chapter first. Then you can rejoin us here.

You will do fine.

Get the Facts Right

Two different general types of information need to be included in your funding application. The first are *objective data,* briefly stated (your name, address, the title of your project, list of potential outside reviewers with their positions and addresses, and so on). Much of this information is entered directly onto the application form—either online, in a downloaded document, or in hard copy, depending on the funding agency. Some of this kind of information—such as the list of references cited in your proposal, the degrees and prizes received by your fellow investigators, or the name of a consulting company you will be using—may appear on attachments or may be embedded in the text itself.

The other kind of information is the *descriptive text* that goes into your project summary, research-program description, biographies, budget-justification pages, and any other prose attachments.

You approach the application differently depending on whether you are inputting data or composing text.

When it comes to recording data, you need to get it right the first time. You cannot risk an error. Therefore, *whenever* you are copying dates, journal page numbers, names of individuals, titles of articles, formulae, and the like into your application, check and double-check right from the beginning to ensure accuracy. You may very well skim over these sections later, when you are proofreading, and because they look and sound right, you may fail to notice that you have inadvertently announced that you published your first paper before you were born or misspelled the name of the leading expert in your field.

Note that spelling names correctly can be crucial to the impression you make with your reviewers and should be attended to with great care in everything you do as an academic. There are many, many researchers in the world, in your own and related fields, and confusion can easily result if you are not precise about surnames and initials. Further, if you misspell the name of a star in your field, your error will serve as a warning sign to particularly picky reviewers of various character defects you did not even know you had. Pay particular attention not only to names that may seem foreign and complex to you but also to those that may be so familiar you do not even feel the urge to check. There are many different spellings of O'Neill, and the Macintoshes and Macmillans of this world can be particular about whether or not you capitalize the I's and M's in the middle of their surnames.

The First Draft of the Text

With the prose sections, you can take a different approach. Here, nothing is written in stone the first time through. You will be editing and reediting, cutting and trimming, possibly moving information from one section to another as you develop and refine the proposal. So, go ahead, be windy and imprecise in the first draft. Later, you will work with these sections until they reach a level of concision and precision that will leave your reviewers wide-eyed with admiration.

Having enough visual space on the computer screen to draft and revise the prose sections is helpful. For this reason, most applicants find it useful (and less stressful) to compose these pieces in a text document; then, when the text is finished, they copy and paste it into the application, rather than trying to create convincing prose right in those little boxes and numbered pages that are provided in most computer-generated application forms. Editing a passage in a text box can be a frustrating experience, as we watch the page breaks move around, fonts change, and margins move from one paragraph to the next—apparently according to the capricious inclinations of some program designer far away. Such mechanical problems can leave you open to error and even cause important material to disappear. More importantly, they require you to think about whether the wheels are staying on the vehicle when you should be concentrating on the driving.

Damn the Torpedoes: Get It Down

Still keeping in mind that the first draft and the final draft are going to be two entirely different things (even if you do only have 24 hours in which to get it done), you need to give yourself permission to "write long" at the beginning. You may have allowed only six pages for the description of your methodology, and you may produce nine or ten pages in your first draft. Later you can cut this down to suit the length required.

Here is how to do the first draft of the project description.

Create a list of headings that is drawn from the topics the funding agency requires you to address, plus any other points you have decided to include. (See chapter 4 for a list of statements to help you to brainstorm material for these headings at the prewriting stage.) Depending on how you prefer to work, you may wish to use a different text file for each of these headings and then merge the files into one master narrative.

Examples of headings include:

- Introduction. An introduction should do what it says: Introduce. Your readers essentially know nothing—certainly nothing substantial—about your project until they read this paragraph. You want to set the stage by being clear and precise, and you want to capture their interest. The introductory paragraph (it is normally just one paragraph) does not cover the same territory as the project summary or abstract (See "A Note Regarding Project Summaries," below). The project summary or abstract, which is a separate section of the application, attempts to encapsulate everything in a few sentences.

The tendency to procrastinate is a problem for almost all of us at some point in our lives. A number of researchers (who obviously overcame it long enough to get their funding applications in on time) are currently investigating why this tendency is rampant among those who are faced with academic deadlines. From the writing (or marking!) of undergraduate term papers, to studying for exams, to finishing master's and doctoral theses, to preparing papers for journal submission, to drafting funding applications, the tendency to procrastinate is a problem of near epidemic proportion in the world of academe. People who are All But Thesis (ABT, also known as ABD, for "All But Dissertation" or, more sardonically, "All But Done") are individuals who have embarked on graduate degrees but have never been able (at least not yet) to finish the written component.

There are many excellent resources for those who are plagued by procrastination either occasionally or chronically. Several of these are listed in the annotated bibliography. I especially recommend the website of the Procrastination Research Group at Carleton University.

For the purposes of getting your grant application done, here are three tips that can help you to surmount procrastination on a temporary basis.

1. *Know what you want to say.* Create an outline and detailed notes for each section of the proposal before you start. If you really want to beat the hesitation blues, you can get even more specific and compose your next sentence in your head before you sit down at the computer—on your way back from coffee, for example, or while you are slicing radishes. Simply type that sentence when you open the computer file, and you will be off and running.

2. *Build on a sound structure.* Many problems with procrastination are caused by an awareness that the emperor is not wearing very many clothes. In the case of research proposals, sometimes the writer knows there are significant problems with the experimental design, the hypothesis to be tested, or even the subject matter that is being investigated, but he or she hopes that by writing well enough, the structural problem will become less obvious—if not invisible. This never happens. If there is a fundamental problem with the project you are proposing, you need to address it before you write anything about it to a funding agency.

3. *Be confident.* With a solid structure beneath you and a clear sense of what you need and want to say, you will find that the tendency to procrastinate evaporates. Solid preparation and knowledge of the material lead to confidence—and confidence is the most powerful weapon there is in the war against delay.

The introductory paragraph sets the tone and establishes the context. It takes the reader from the external world with all of its distractions into the world of your research.

- Importance of your project to (a) your field, (b) your discipline, (c) the world (context, setting, rationale).
- Summary of what is known on the subject already (literature review).
- Description of the research investigation. Describe step by step how you are going to carry out the work and, where indicated, why you have chosen the experimental method or instrument you have chosen (methodology).
- Data analysis. You must show in advance that you know exactly how you are going to determine the outcome of your study. This is true no matter how early in the course of your research project you are applying. Many reviewers say that the plans for data analysis are where grant applicants tend to be most sloppy. Some people on a grant-selection committee have been chosen because of their expertise and experience in data analysis, and they will look for oversights and errors.
- Why you? Why here? Why now? What relevant experience and knowledge do you have that makes you the best person or group to carry out this project? What have you achieved with any funding you have received in the past? What are the advantages of your research environment? Why are you well situated in time (both in terms of your career as a researcher, and in terms of this moment in history vis-à-vis your area of research focus) and location (proximity of specific expertise in related fields, or to certain facilities such as a synchrotron) to carry out the work?
- Plans for disseminating your findings, transferring knowledge to clinical settings, and so on.
- How the project fits with the agency's or program's funding mandate.

- Potential side benefits of your research (training and education of students; community involvement, etc.).
- Conclusion. In a separate paragraph, end the piece on a strong note. Your concluding paragraph may be a summary, or it may look beyond the time frame of the current project by explaining the future research it could lead to. Think of yourself as having picked up your readers in a limousine in the introductory paragraph and taken them on a tour of your project. Now it is time to drop them off again. You do not want to be abrupt. You want to leave them feeling satisfied about what they have seen, and as though you have returned them with confidence to the external world.

Not all funding applications require the same information. You need to tailor this list to the specific application you are working on—by adding points to as well as removing points from different sections, in order to match your outline to the agency's requirements.

Now that you have the list of headings, do the following:

1. Write down (or cut and paste) under each heading every point you can think of that belongs under that heading; then
2. Reorder the headings if necessary in order to attain the most logical presentation for this particular application; then
3. Double check that every point you have listed under each heading belongs under the heading where you have put it; then
4. Add any additional information you may have overlooked; then
5. Write the material under each heading into a paragraph; then, finally—
6. Presto! Zippo! Take out the headings.

Note: If there is more than one prose section (for example, if "Project Description" and "Investigator Biographies" are two separate prose sections), you will save time and avoid duplication or inappropriate placement of information if you repeat steps 1 through 3 for each section before completing steps 4 and 5 for each section.

After following these steps, you will be left with a coherent, well organized, useful document, almost like ripping a tablecloth out from under a table setting, leaving all the plates and cutlery neatly sitting on the glass table, properly aligned.

Again, expect your document to be too long at this stage. In addition, after the headings have been taken out you may need to recast a few sentences at the start of a paragraph here and there, providing transitions so readers can follow the flow of the text. You may also need to change the order of some sentences and/or to add new bits of text to make your paragraphs work together more smoothly and your ideas unfold in a more logical manner. This, of course, will make the document longer yet. Do not worry: cutting text is always easier than creating it. (And the following chapters tell you how.)

A Note Regarding Project Summaries

Some funding applications request a short description or summary of the research project (it may be referred to as a *proposal abstract*). It usually appears on a separate page before the main narrative begins. The agency normally specifies a word limit for the project summary—two hundred words, for example.

In the project summary, you need to be as succinct as possible while also ensuring accuracy. Your goal is to attract the attention and interest of your readers, encouraging them to want to read the rest of your application. As well as briefly describing the purpose of your study and the form it will take, the summary should, if appropriate (that is, without inflating the actual potential impact of your work), provide a global context for your research and point out its implications.

Even when it is referred to as an abstract, a project summary in a funding application is not the same as a journal abstract. An abstract for a journal or a book of conference proceedings is intended as a summary of the content of your text, provided to allow readers to determine—without having to read the entire piece—whether it is relevant to their own areas of interest. A journal abstract is normally addressed to the initiated. In a grant application, on the other hand, you need to avoid deeply technical language that will be difficult for scholars who are not specialists in your field to understand.

Depending on the funding agency's practices, you may also want to keep the lay reader in mind. Some granting organizations cut and paste the project summaries of successful applications into media releases or other public communications, or at least make this information available to the public on request. If a reporter may at some point base an interview with you on what you have written in your project summary—or even write an article without bothering to interview you—it may be worth the extra time to ensure clarity for the nonacademic reader.

For a sample project summary, please see appendix B.

8

GET IT RIGHT
The Second Draft

· ·

Now that you have created a first draft, you need to review what you have written and then move sentences or paragraphs around for the most effective organization, substantiate points where necessary so your arguments are strong and persuasive, and check to make sure that you have not omitted anything important.

Focus only on *content* this time through. You need to be objective about what you have written in the first draft—but only in terms of its logical development and substance. Within reason, do not be concerned just yet about whether the document is too long, or worry too much now about making improvements to style or language. All that fine tuning will come in the next (a.k.a. the "final") draft.

Now is the time to closely consider these aspects of the proposal:

- Title
- Opening Statement
- Soundness of Arguments
- Logical Development
- Concluding Statement

✎

In order to create effective explanatory prose, you need to take the mental focus off yourself and put it on the reader. ▮

The Title

The title should be "short and sweet"—as succinct and as descriptive as possible. It should reflect the actual subject matter of the research without going into too much detail. For example, "Life on Other Planets" is too general, while "A Three-Year Preliminary Program That Will Contribute to the Groundwork in the Search for Earth-Like Planets by Finding Sun-Like Stars through the Use of a 75-m Interferometer, Resolution-Correction Telescopes, and Seven Other Instruments" is too specific (and too long).

When developing your title, do not overlook the power of a colon. Those two little dots can help you engage the interest of your readers before you get into the more substantial description. It can also set the tone for the work to follow and even inject some humor if you feel it is appropriate. Titles of full-length works of nonfiction often make excellent use of this technique, some examples being *The Tipping Point: How Little Things Can Make a Big Difference* (by Malcolm Gladwell), *Eats, Shoots and Leaves: The Zero Tolerance Approach to Punctuation* (Lynne Truss), *Freakonomics: A Rogue Economist Explores the Hidden Side of Everything* (Steven D. Levitt and Stephen J. Dubner), and *The Happiness Hypothesis: Finding Modern Truth in Ancient Wisdom* (Jonathan Haidt).

A good way to discover what you think works and does not work in titles is to develop the habit of scrutinizing the titles of the research projects, books, and scholarly papers you encounter in your reading. You can base your own titles on others that appeal to you, too, because titles are about the only component of writing projects that are not copyrightable. So go ahead and call your project "Moby Dick" if you think it will add to its impact.

Do not stir up controversy with the title or the short description of your project. Particularly when the granting agency gets some or all of its funding from government sources, or in other direct or indirect ways from public funds, its critics and political opponents enjoy nothing more than publicizing the names of funded research projects that sound ridiculous or outrageous to the uninitiated—or that might be interpreted as immoral by someone. If you are conducting a survey into the ways in which the female breast is depicted in pre-twentieth-century works of art, or are undertaking an investigation into the physical benefits of smoking, you may want to summarize your subject matter obliquely or at least sensitively—although, of course, still accurately—in the title and short description. Through the perceptive deployment of language, you can help the granting agency avoid direct attacks if they decide to fund your work—or at least you can help to alleviate their concerns about incurring public censure. Consider that for the two examples above, such titles as "Depictions of the Female among the Impressionists" and "The Effects of Nicotine on Mental Focus: A Silver Lining in a Deadly Cloud" are viable possibilities.

Such cautions do not, of course, apply to the actual description of the research: in the description, specificity is crucially important.

Opening Statement

Now you will turn your attention to revising the main section of the application, where you provide the detailed description of the research. You may have been allowed anywhere from four to sixteen pages for this section.

You need to come strongly out of the starting gate with a powerful introduction. Here you state what is, to you, obvious—not only the "what" but the "why." In the first paragraph you should situate your project for the reviewer, show your enthusiasm, and engage the reader's interest.

Rather than this:

I am writing to apply for funding for a project that ten of my colleagues and I are undertaking that builds on our more than sixty collective years of hardwood and insect investigation. Our team, which consists of scientists from eight different universities and four disciplines, and ranges from doctoral students to award-winning full professors, intends to examine the possible effects of increasing average temperatures in the aspen parkland in northern North America on the population increments and diminishments among *Malacosoma disstria* and their feeding patterns vis-à-vis *Populus tremula*.

Say this:

> For decades prior to 1990, periods of defoliation of hardwoods by tent caterpillars (*Malacosoma disstria*) occurred in cycles approximately seven years in length. But in Location X between 1995 and 2005, rather than fluctuating, the populations of *M. disstria* steadily decreased. The purpose of our current investigation is to determine the causes of the decrease in population of *M. disstria* in Location X during this time period, including possible connections to climate change. We intend to project the long-term impact on hardwoods in general and the European aspen (*Populus tremula*) in particular.

The first example, while clear enough from a structural perspective, suffers from navel gazing; we wonder whether the researchers are aware of the world beyond their area of investigation. Their description is also boring. Even those who come to the table with a consuming interest in tent caterpillars or aspens are likely to ask "So what?"

The second description is much better oriented toward a range of potential readers. It is written in clear language, provides context for the research, and stimulates the reader's interest.

Try reading your description to someone from outside your field. If they understand what you are talking about (or, better yet, say, "Cool!"), you will know that you have achieved your goal.

Strengthen Your Arguments

Many applications for scholarly funding are turned down because the arguments intended to support them are unsound, weak, or confusing. While most reviewers are honorable and kind, not all of them are saints. They take well-deserved pride in their strengths in intellectual investigation, and such pride can sometimes manifest itself as delight in finding gaps and flaws in applicants' thinking—and in pointing them out to other members of the panel. Do not put yourself in a position to be skewered—or even to have your proposal regretfully passed over—because of a minor oversight or error.

Review your material closely, looking for any problems that may interfere with reviewers' understanding of what you are going to do, how you are going to do it, and why you need to do it. Answer any potential questions about your project that may arise when reviewers are considering your application. You will not be there to answer in person.

- *Look for statements that need support or evidence.* Take particular note of statements about matters of common knowledge to researchers in your own field that may be unfamiliar to nonspecialists. (Use your judgment here. For example, "Not everyone who tests positive for HIV will ultimately develop AIDS" would benefit from a citation, while "Cumulonimbus clouds are associated with electrical storms" may not.)
- *Identify your underlying assumptions.* Let us say you intend to compare the incidence of tooth decay in people who live in communities where the water is naturally fluoridated with that of people living in communities with artificially fluoridated water. Clearly, your study is based on an assumption that fluoride in water prevents cavities in teeth. Since not everyone agrees with that assumption, you need to acknowledge the premise from which you have started and to support your position with references.
- *Address potential problems that may arise during the research.* What if you are unable to gather sufficient data during fieldwork to prove or disprove your hypothesis? What is your alternative plan? Can you use raw data from other studies?

Can you go back to the field at some later time and try again? Can you use another method of analysis? While it is impossible (and pointless) to try to anticipate every eventuality that could arise during a research study, it is also necessary to be realistic.

- *Show the need for your work.* While applicants should always situate specific projects in a larger context for reviewers, doing so is particularly necessary if your project appears for any reason not to be distinctive. You need to show exactly how your work is different from what is already out there. Ideally, you cite the literature that comes closest to your study, and then point out that none of the research just cited has considered an important issue—which is (ta-da!) the *very question* that you are intending to address.

- *Anticipate objections.* If your project is unusually large or complex, prepare for the reviewer who will say, "She's crazy if she thinks she can do all this in a three-year study." Address such potential concerns in the application by stating, for example, "The work I propose to do here is an important component of a larger ten-year study. Clearly, the scope of this topic is greater than what can be accomplished in three years. However, by focusing on points A, B and C, I will make tangible progress that will form the foundation for subsequent research by me, my colleagues, and others in the field."

- *Show your muscle.* You want the reviewers to know that you are the ideal person (or team) to be carrying out this work at this time. You cannot be certain that reviewers will read your CVs, and they may even skim your biographies. Therefore if you or your co-investigators have one or several publications in leading research journals, point these out in the text of your proposal. If you have won research awards, mention them in the text. If you have made specific contributions to training qualified people in your field, or to knowledge transfer, do not leave it to the review panel to figure out this information for themselves from the contents of your CV. They probably will not. Put it in the text.

- *Show that you can do what you say you can do.* To do this you must make sure that your credentials are clearly set out in your application. You may also need to explain what ongoing initiatives (committee work, society executive positions) you intend to put on hold or curtail, or what help you are planning to enlist, in order to carry out the project within the projected time frame.

- *Describe your network of support.* Where appropriate, indicate why the university or research center where you will carry out your work is an ideal location for such investigation—due to its geographical location, technical resources, institutional support for your area of study, and other reasons. You will also want to explain why the members of your team are ideal complements to one another and to you, based on their background and experience, research interests, qualifications, seniority and stature in their field, and other attributes, and explain how each member of the team will contribute to the work at hand.

Logic, Logic, Logic

A must lead to B must lead to C. Double-check that one statement leads to another and gradually builds your case. (Refer to chapter 4 for more information on the subject of logic.) Assessing the logical development of your arguments could include such mechanical exercises as making sure that the studies you cite to make a specific point are presented in chronological order or, if they are not, that there was an organizational reason for a nonchronological approach.

Concluding Statement

In a grant application you don't normally have a lot of space to conclude your presentation, but even if you have only one sentence, make it a strong one. Avoid ending in medias res—in the middle of things (for example, "All participants signed an informed-consent statement," or "These results are likely to be applicable to other species of venomous snake"). You want to encapsulate—or at least conclude—like this: "Such initiatives are intended to improve the accuracy of the diagnostic process, ultimately benefiting all patients," or "This research will add a critical dimension to our understanding of the work of this important filmmaker."

Rather than wobbling to a stop, continue to show power as you zoom across the finish line.

9

GET IT SMOOTH
The Final Draft

···

The time has come to worry about everything you have not
yet worried about.

On this, your final significant revision of the manuscript,
you need to focus on the particular. You need to cut unnecessary
words, phrases, and sentences, eliminate repetition, and make sure
that your message is expressed clearly and consistently.

An Appeal with Appeal

For many years there has been a widespread misconception that
scholarly writing must be formal, dense, and complex in order to be
considered authoritative. Today many academics are moving away
from this mindset in an effort to disseminate the results of their
scholarship more broadly and to draw more readers to their work.
Scholars who are working to engage the reader more fully in their
writing may wish to look for guidance to writers whose primary focus is on telling a story—novelists and playwrights, for example.

Like good fiction (not to mention the more interesting aspects of
life itself), much scholarly investigation arises from conflict—and
conflict is the foundation upon which engrossing prose is built. The
conflict that forms the basis for research can often be expressed like
this: "We always thought A, but now that we know about B (or 'now

that B has changed,' or 'if we deliberately change B'), it becomes necessary for us to revisit, reevaluate, reconsider, and/or retest some of our former assumptions."

All interesting writing—whether in a novel or a research paper—contains enough elements of good storytelling to attract readers' attention in the first paragraph, keep them interested through the body of the work, and leave them satisfied with the conclusion. Obviously, this effect must be achieved without compromising objectivity and accuracy; notwithstanding this basic tenet, a grant proposal can be written so that readers (in this case, the reviewers) will be cheering for you (the hero of the tale) as you take on your battle on behalf of humanity to wrest enlightenment and order from the forces of ignorance and faulty reasoning.

To engage your readers in this way, you must start with a statement that not only summarizes what you intend to do but also reflects your enthusiasm for your research. Your description of the proposed project (which is already well organized, thanks to your work on earlier drafts) needs to sustain enthusiasm or energy, and deliver it straight through to the conclusion.

Attend to the Details

As you go through your final draft, focus on your use of language. You want to make your presentation as clear and strong as possible. If you confuse your readers with convoluted sentences and obscure vocabulary, you create a swamp for reviewers to wade through before they can even begin to consider the value of your proposal.

- Use simple, straightforward language. Do not use words that are overly technical or esoteric or that sound "affected."
- Define technical or unfamiliar terms for intelligent reviewers who are not in your specific research area.
- Check the facts. Double-check all dates, citations and numerical information for accuracy. Do not rely on your memory.

FINDING EDITING ASSISTANCE

Scholars who are unsure of their own capacities for strong written presentations often find it helpful to seek outside assistance with the final drafts of papers and funding applications. This is particularly true of researchers whose first language is not the one in which they are making their submissions.

If you require an editor, first check out what resources are available on campus to help you. Many universities have writing centers that are staffed by students and faculty with proficiency in editing. Some scholars feel awkward taking advantage of such services, but there is no need to feel this way. (For some reason, no one who is unable to calculate a square root in their heads worries about asking for help with *that,* but most of us feel as though we should be able to sort out tricky grammatical constructions and know exactly how to use a semicolon.) If all else fails, a professional editor can be a good investment—of time as well as money. Unlike major substantive editing, basic proofing and copyediting services do not generally cost very much.

Your first choice in identifying a professional editor should be to get a referral, but you can also look for editors and editors' associations in the phone book or online. If you don't know someone personally who has used the specific editor, insist on seeing a resume or curriculum vitae and follow up with a couple of calls to former clients to confirm that he or she is likely to do an excellent job—and get the work done on time.

Good editing requires intelligence, an obsessive love of language (with a particular focus on language as a communications tool), human-relations skills, and a respect for deadlines. Far too many people who are not good editors hang up shingles claiming that they are. Caveat emptor.

- Use the allocated space. If the guidelines allow you twelve pages of text, use them.

Avoid the following:

- Long, convoluted statements. Keep your sentences relatively short and clear.
- Jargon. Jargon may confuse reviewers (not to mention make their eyes glaze over). Sociologists are not familiar with all of the terminology of economists, and vice versa. You need to

find ways to say things that are clear to all potential reviewers, whether they are in your field or not.

- Acronyms. Again, certain acronyms may mean something in your field but may mean nothing (or, worse, mean something else) in the field of the reviewer. When you use acronyms that are not familiar to your reviewers, they will probably need to search back through your document to find the first time the term was spelled out in full. Doing this is like consulting a foreign-language dictionary while asking directions: it is time-consuming and frustrating. Some acronyms are in common usage (such as NIH in the United States, NSERC in Canada, MRC in Great Britain, and AIDS anywhere), and some presentations need to use an acronym repeatedly (in which case the reviewer will undoubtedly learn its meaning). If you use an acronym only infrequently in your presentation, however, try instead to use a word or a phrase to describe what you mean. (Some perspective can be gained on the range of possibilities that can arise from a single acronym by plugging your acronym into an acronym definer on the Internet. One of them lists seventy-one entries for SNAP—including "Stop Needless Acronym Proliferation").

- Overly long descriptive phrases that you need to repeat over and over again. Let us say one group in your study includes a hospital's physicians, nurses, physiotherapists, and occupational therapists. The other group includes the hospital's lawyers and accountants. Choose a term that captures the spirit of each list and use it in subsequent references to the group, rather than listing all of its constituent members each time. For example, you could say "The first group will include physicians, nurses, physiotherapists, and occupational therapists (the 'Health Professionals'), while the second group is made up of the hospital's lawyers and accountants (the 'Administrative Professionals')." Less elegantly, you could define the first group as Group A and the second as Group B. The goal is to avoid repetition of overly long lists or phrases.

Too Long?

If your descriptive materials are too long for the allocated space, you cannot use a type size that is smaller than specified or make your margins narrower than the guidelines allow. (Note that many agencies also forbid the use of fonts that are, by design, smaller than standard fonts.) Nor is it wise to submit four pages when you have been permitted three in the hope that you will be given some latitude by your reviewers. Some funding agencies remove pages from applications that exceed the specified limit before sending the packages to reviewers, and you must assume that this is what the agency you are applying to will do.

If the text of your submission is too long, there are only two things you can do:

1. *Eliminate repetition.* You do not have room to repeat yourself. Grant applications do not provide you with the leeway to say the same thing in two different ways (or three, as I have just done here).
2. *Cut extraneous material.* If it is not on topic, take it out. This is true of words as well as sentences and paragraphs. For example, the sentence

   From the beginning, the efforts of John Boyd-Smith made an essential contribution to the support effort in the development of the hockey team that would ultimately go on to win the first Marley Cup for the university.

can be trimmed to read

   John Boyd-Smith made an essential contribution to the university's first Marley Cup–winning hockey team.

The second version eliminates two-thirds of the words.

Your interpretation of what is repetitious and what is extraneous is likely to vary depending on how many words you need to trim. Your editing efforts will range from making minor changes to major revisions that may threaten the cohesiveness of your entire narrative. In the latter case you may need to go back and reorganize the whole document in order to present it more succinctly while still preserving its comprehensiveness and clarity.

Proof and Be Proofed

The last stage of writing anything, of course, is to proofread it. Writers generally proofread their own work best when they put the document away for a week or so and get some mental distance from it. Most grant applicants do not have this kind of time. If you do, or even if you do not, one effective way of checking for omitted words or awkward sentence structure is to read the text aloud. However or whenever you do it, proofreading is essential.

After you have proofread the material yourself, pass the document to someone you believe is qualified to look at it from a purely language perspective—perhaps a friend or relative who has not looked at it before. Even if you are yourself a master of spelling and grammar, you should still get someone to read your application through before you submit it.

If you are not a language expert, find someone who is. Good spelling and good grammar are critically important to your presentation, and a source of good spelling and good grammar is not that hard to secure. Mentally go through your circle of friends and colleagues and try to identify a capable proofreader who will be sympathetic (you don't need an obsessive nitpicker who can do everything better than everyone else) but who will also be firm enough to communicate any real shortcomings, oversights, or errors in your prose.

10

GET IT DONE

Review, Refresh, Release

....

Y ou are now ready to receive an informal review of your funding application from a reader with scholarly expertise. As I explained more fully in chapter 2, this individual is likely to be a colleague in a field related to yours (but not in the same field) with experience in writing successful grant applications—in other words, someone who can give you an informed and objective report on what you have written from the point of view of one of your future actual reviewers. Ideally, the feedback you receive will indicate such problems as fuzzy or faulty thinking, lack of connective "tissue" between components of your research (or between your research and the research of others), unsubstantiated assumptions, or missing citations.

Because of the type of informed feedback you want at this point, you need to give your expert critic a complete application. Otherwise, no matter how clearly you explain where you intend to add additional material later, you deprive your first reviewer of salient information that you yourself will think of only when you get the last parts filled in. Gaps also interrupt the flow of your presentation and reduce its overall impact. In short, you diminish the potential contribution of someone who can give you valuable advice.

Ideally, you contact your expert reviewer several weeks or even months before you expect to complete the application, to secure his or her assistance ahead of time. Ideally, too, you send the document to the expert reviewer about four to six weeks before the funding agency's deadline (or your in-house institutional deadline). This schedule allows plenty of time for your informal reviewer to read your application and provide you with feedback, and for you to consider and incorporate suggested revisions or additions.

If the length of time left before the deadline is less than ideal, try to compensate at your end rather than asking your reviewer to do so. If only one week remains, for example, give the reviewer five days to appraise the application and allow yourself only two for final revisions. Your colleague's workload is undoubtedly as heavy as yours, and he or she will need to carve out time to do this job for you. You want to predispose this person to approach the task in a helpful frame of mind, so be generous.

On a related note, be grateful and gracious. Send a thank-you note to your informal reviewer, and perhaps take him or her to lunch. But also accept the advice—or at least give it serious consideration—and let the reviewer know that you have done so. Refrain from arguing with expert reviewers who have volunteered their time to help you— unless you are certain you never want them to assist you in that capacity again.

One Last Look

Content counts most, but the physical appearance of your application will influence the reviewers at the funding agency as well. It is far too easy for them to assume that a person who is sloppy when it comes to the layout of an application is also the type of person who may take shortcuts in research or on a literature review. A panel of experts can come to erroneous conclusions based on appearances. Do not give them the opportunity to do so.

After you have incorporated editorial changes and reviewers' feedback and proofread your submission for the final time, you need to do the following.

1. Skim your document. Sit it up straight if you are skimming text in hard copy, or sit back from the screen if it is an online submission. Let your eyes slide over the pages (or over the screen as you scroll down), looking for paragraphs that break halfway through, margins that zigzag across the document, or text that suddenly changes font or type size.

2. Review any attachments, such as copies of journal articles and your CV. Make sure that they are all where they should be, that no pages are missing, that they are properly collated (that the pages appear in the proper order), and that they are either stapled or paper-clipped as required.

3. Review the grant-submission guidelines one last time to make sure that you are sending the correct number of copies (where applicable) and that your application adheres to the required format.

4. Package hard-copy materials neatly and in such a way that they are not likely to be bent, folded, or mangled en route. After all your work on this application, go ahead and take a few extra minutes to make sure that your submission looks as professional and polished as it sounds.

Sloppy appearance can undermine the most scholarly of arguments. To quote one experienced reviewer, applicants should "avoid looking like what they actually are—rushed, harried people doing rushed, harried work." ▌▌

Let It Go!

While most of us have trouble getting everything done that needs to be done before a grant-application deadline, some people do finish their applications early. And even then they may have trouble letting them go.

At a certain point you need to admit to yourself that your work on this proposal is finished, that revising material too often can make it worse instead of better, and that it is time for you to get this package off your desk or desktop and move on to other things. When you reach this point, sure, go ahead and utter magical incantations and follow superstitious rituals if you like. But then send the application on its way.

What Happens Next?

When your work is done, the work of the funding agency in determining the outcome of your application begins.

In most cases, when your submission reaches the agency, it first is looked over by one of the agency's grants administrators. This person makes sure that your application is eligible for consideration under the agency's guidelines for that particular competition and that you have included all the necessary documents. Grants officers routinely assign a number to the submission. Many of them advise the applicant that the application has reached the agency, and that it is complete. These are also the people who locate any letters that your referees have submitted directly to the granting agency, and they attach those letters to your materials.

Once the initial processing requirements are complete, agency personnel send the reviewers copies of all applications to be considered in the designated round. (Increasingly, this process is being done online, in order to save time and paper. The FastLane system at the National Science Foundation is a leading example.) In some cases the reviewers are members of a standing committee who have been appointed for several-year terms; in other cases, some or all of them are selected after all funding applications have been received, to eliminate the possibility that any applicants are asked to be reviewers.

In addition to sending packages to panel members, agency administrators begin to get in touch with expert outside readers as directed or as indicated by the circumstances and to send those readers copies of the documents they need to review. When it comes to outside readers, some agencies take the advice of the applicants. On the other hand, it is rumored that some agencies choose anyone *other than* the readers the applicant has suggested. Most agencies have a protocol that balances outside readers recommended by applicants with those selected by review panels or senior agency administrators.

After a specified time during which review panelists and outside experts assess the submissions (often against a set of prespecified criteria), a meeting of the reviewers is convened. Typically, each reviewer arrives at the meeting with each application temporarily classified into one of three categories: "definitely fund," "definitely do not fund," or "for discussion" (a.k.a., "Yes," "No," or "Maybe"). In addition to classifying the submissions, each reviewer has made a note of the rationale for each classification.

Although reviewers for major funding agencies may discuss only a certain percentage of the applications, they may send individual comments to some or all of the other applicants that will help them revise their applications to improve their chances for success in the next round.

Of course, seldom do all the reviewers agree on who should be funded and who should not—and even if they did agree, there probably would not be enough money to fund all the deserving applicants. In order to reach a consensus, meetings of grant review panels can go on for several days. Were it not for the fact that these meetings are moderated by senior agency staff whose abilities include skills in conflict resolution, they might go on for weeks!

Some agencies tell reviewing panels how many projects can be supported only after agreement has been reached on which projects should be funded, and in what order of priority. Thus it happens, for example, that reviewers learn after the fact that only seven on their unanimous top ten list will actually receive grants. Most agencies introduce a dollar figure (or a number of fundable projects, if the grant amount is fixed) once the majority of applications have been eliminated, and the committee is then required to reach its consensus with this information at hand. Other agencies refer the reviewers' prioritized list of applicants to another committee, which then makes the final decisions on funding allocation.

Reviewers often would like to approve more applications than can be funded by the available money, which means that they or the agency must either eliminate projects they would very much like to fund, or start tweaking applicants' budgets (and most people believe that no one wins once budget tweaking begins). Occasionally, there are fewer deserving applicants than there is money, which puts the reviewers in almost as awkward a position: as researchers themselves, they know that if they do not give all the money away, they jeopardize the funding system—because the amount of available funds may be decreased in response to the apparent lack of demand. (This is another good reason why scholars must develop truly valuable research projects and outstanding grant proposals: by doing so, they contribute to the process of funding scholarly and scientific research.)

The process may not be finished even after the review panel has met. Often there is a meeting of the executive committee or board, which must sanction review-panel decisions before the outcome becomes official. Such approvals usually amount to rubber-stamping, but nothing is ever over until it's over. Any legitimate part of the process can change the outcome. If you hear rumors that the jury has met and you have been approved, it is wise not to start counting chickens, hiring consultants, or calling the local news media—yet. Once you receive a letter with an official signature on it (or some equally binding document), then you can tell the world that your funding has been approved.

11

CLOSE THE CIRCLE

Some scholars put absolutely everything into the effort of writing a grant proposal—neglecting their other work, their families, even their hygiene, and incurring the wrath of collaborators and junior researchers who are forced to burn the midnight oil in support of these individuals' efforts to create perfect applications. Other scholars believe it is so utterly obvious that either they or their projects merit funding that they needn't waste much energy on fine-tuning their proposals. Members of these groups tend to be flabbergasted when they receive a rejection from the agency. They immediately decide to appeal the decision, sink into a debilitating depression, or both.

On the other side of the hall, some scholars are so negative about their odds of success that despite having created excellent and comprehensive funding applications, they are unprepared for positive results. By the time they receive their letters of approval, these individuals may already have collapsed their own programs into someone else's research or become buried in unrelated commitments. Although those who unexpectedly succeed may ultimately be happier than those who are surprised to learn that they did not, neither approach is rational. Agencies' success rates for funding applications vary widely, and nothing is for sure. Wisdom suggests keeping your life and your mind open to deal with either eventuality.

All right. At this point your project has either been approved or it has not. What do you do now?

Since the rejection end of the results spectrum may not be black and white, whereas acceptance usually is, and since rejection is more likely than acceptance, we will look at that potential outcome first.

Oh, No: Dealing with Rejection

Of course, a "No" from a funding agency is not always an out-and-out rejection, but it does feel like it when you receive that "Sorry, but no thank you" letter. Some applicants experience the mixed blessing of being advised that their projects were of sufficient merit that they would have been funded had there been more money available for grants, but more often a negative response comes by way of a form letter that says, for example,

> We received many excellent applications and could not fund them all. We regret to inform you that yours was not among the successful projects during the most recent review cycle.

The letter may be accompanied by feedback from reviewers and may close by saying something like "We encourage you to apply again next time" or (less encouragingly) "We wish you success with obtaining funding for your project elsewhere."

The best thing to do right after you receive a negative response to a funding application is: nothing. Let the outcome stumble around in your head for a while before taking any action. You need to assimilate the bad news—let the sharp edges get a bit worn down. (They *will* wear down.) But do not leave the matter unattended for too long, or you may never find the courage to deal with it. After a few days, get the application out and put it on your desk or desktop and start to decide what you want to do about it.

Your first job is to find out why your proposal was turned down. It is human nature to feel that a negative response means that the entire project has been rejected, and then to reflect that it is no wonder your proposal was rejected (it deserved nothing more than total rejection), and then to decide that you yourself are also worthy of rejection and should give up your career immediately—when in fact the review committee may have found only one small component of your application to be weak or unacceptable.

To get a start on understanding why your application was declined, reread the comments from the reviewers. If you did not receive comments from reviewers, contact the agency to find out whether any specific feedback on your application can be made available. Reread the comments calmly and with a view to using them as constructive criticism.

If you learn that you have been rejected out of hand (that is, your application landed in the original "Do not fund" pile and stayed there), it is generally a waste of time to try to revise and resubmit your proposal—at least to that agency. A flat-out negative response usually indicates that there is a basic problem with the funding application. You need to find out what that problem is.

If you do not have specific or useful guidance in the form of reviewers' comments, read the proposal again yourself to try to discover whether there is a significant disconnect with the agency's guidelines, or whether you have overlooked something obvious in the budget. Perhaps you will suddenly see an error in the experiment's design. If the agency does not offer any guidance, try to get a reading from a fresh set of eyes in your circle of colleagues.

In cases of out-and-out rejection, you must find out what caused your proposal to be turned down before you try to do anything with it. Even if you realize that the only explanation for your lack of success is that you were reviewed by the "wrong" jury for political or other reasons, you will be able to move forward with some logical purpose in deciding what your next step ought to be, instead of shooting more arrows into the night. Even if you believe the reviewers were utterly wrong on every point, you need to accept responsibility and revise your application so that they do not make the same mistake the next time you submit.

Yes? No? Maybe So

If comments have been forwarded to you from the review panel explaining your lack of success, read the feedback closely. Is there a specific problem you can focus on? Did the jury say that the scope of the project was too extensive, for example—or too narrow? Maybe you failed to provide enough information in a specific area, or one of your letters of reference was unsupportive. When you know what the specific problem is, you will be able to address it.

You must also determine whether you were invited to address a single problem and then to resubmit your application, or were given guidance that essentially requires you to overhaul the whole proposal. If you have been invited to resubmit, it is worthwhile to note in your revised proposal that you have addressed the issues that were previously raised. You want to draw the review panel's attention to the changes you make. Remember that these are busy people, and they need your help and guidance.

If you have not been invited to resubmit, do not respond as if you have. In that case, make a fresh start on your application, keeping what succeeded and changing what did not. You do not want to be rejected again next time just because your application sounded too familiar. Taking a different slant on your investigation often gives not only your research but also the review panel a whole new perspective on the project.

Accentuate the Positive

Rejections can be discouraging, especially after you have spent a lot of time preparing and gathering materials for what you thought was a strong submission. Letters of regret from funding agencies are most distressing to newer researchers and scholars, whose faith in the value of their scholarly activity and their own talents or abilities may be particularly vulnerable.

If you are new to the academic world, you will be reassured to hear that for most people, the ego seems quite naturally to evolve and strengthen over time. Some people do have lingering problems as a result of early rejections, however, and these academics, even midcareer, are often reluctant to apply for grants. You do not want to be in that position. Procrastinating on the next application or giving up the contest altogether are not good ideas.

It is also not a good idea to get (visibly) angry: not about the rejection itself, and not about the specific advice you get from reviewers or others whose opinions you have sought out after receiving the bad news. Pay attention to what they are saying. If you feel it is wise to do so, you may reject in a mature manner any advice you receive, but lashing back will never get you anywhere.

Instead of dwelling on your dreams that did not come true, focus on the benefits you have experienced by applying for the grant. The process has helped to clarify your thinking about your research project, and possibly even about the entire direction of the scholarly investigation on which you are embarked. It may sound trite, but it is true that those who are dealing with a failure to secure funding early in their careers need to remind themselves that they did not learn to ride a bicycle the first time, either. A tremendous skill set is required for successful grant writing. It is necessary to think of early applications in particular as strategies for learning skills that are needed to support a successful lifelong career in research and scholarly activity.

As you already know if you are more than a few years into your academic career, becoming increasingly respected as a researcher simply means that the funding stakes get larger—your chances of success remain similarly daunting. However, you will almost certainly become more accepting of negative outcomes as time passes. The earliest applications are the most difficult; keep in mind that *this* particular application is not the be-all and end-all of your career. *Every* established academic has received rejections for grants and articles at some point; indeed, it is likely that the more established and respected the academic is, the more rejections he or she has received. Nothing ventured? Nothing gained. Put your own short-term failures in context. The experience makes you stronger and tougher—and both of these are qualities you need to get ahead in any competitive environment.

Ultimately, you need to get up off the floor, dust yourself off, and start the application process again. Figure out what you have learned from this experience—and then allow yourself to move on.

Celebrate: Dealing with Success

This section is much shorter than the previous one. Most of us succeed quite well in dealing with success, but we fail miserably in dealing with failure. Isn't that strange?

Before you crack the champagne, though, why not reread your application in light of the approval letter you just received? It may have been months since you submitted it, and you can now give it a fresh look. While your confidence is still high, make yourself notes for the next time you apply for funding. What do you like about this funding proposal, and what do you think appealed to the reviewers? Is there anything you would change for next time?

After the party is over and you have started in to work, keep in mind that your research now has strings attached to it. It is not just yours—it is also partly the property of the funding agency. Be sure you do what you said you would do, when you said you would do it, and ask for permission from the agency if there are any significant variations. Keep your paperwork strictly in order, including receipts and time sheets, and complete interim and final reports and any other follow-up—promptly, and in the format the funding agency requires.

Making excellent use of the funding you have received this time will strengthen your position when you apply next time.

12

BUILD YOUR CREDENTIALS

....

I n the world of academic research and scholarly activity, you are judged largely on your track record, particularly by those who do not know you personally. And unless an agent is managing your career, no one in the universe except you cares about burnishing that record. You may not even care about it yourself most of the time, but you will care a great deal when the time comes to submit the next funding application (or when a colleague down the hall sends you an e-mail that says, "We would like to nominate you for the Chemistry Genius of the Year Award. Can you get your CV to us by Wednesday morning?").

As you become established in your career and increasingly busy—not only with research and publishing but also with teaching and professional service—it becomes more difficult to find the time or inclination to sit down and update your CV. Your curriculum vitae does need to be updated, however—it should contain an entry for every presentation you have given, every committee on which you have served, and every journal article to which your name has been attached (including the correctly spelled names of co-authors and accurately recorded volume and page numbers, not to mention correctly deployed commas and semicolons, italics and capital letters), and so on. Many of us throw our publications in a pile beside the computer, telling ourselves we will enter the information in our CV later. We may also be guilty of reassuring ourselves en route to delivering a keynote address that this is so important an event, we are sure to remember to add it to our CV the next time we get a chance.

And yet many important speeches and publications by many important people never get recorded in their CVs and resumes, due mainly to disorganization and forgetfulness. This is the kind of practical oversight that contributes to the stereotype of the "absentminded professor." Most absentminded professors are not absentminded at all: they are just so focused on their areas of study, and so busy with related activities, that the routines of daily life are of no consequence to them. In other words, it's not that they forget, my dear—they just don't give a damn.

If you are still in the early stages of your career and have not yet reached this state of all-consuming (however productive) distraction, make it a point to establish a tickler system for recording your achievements. (Early is best, but later is better than never, so if you haven't pulled your CV up on your computer since two versions of Word or WordPerfect ago, you need to schedule some time to get caught up.) You may wish to establish a system where your Personal Digital Assistant reminds you on a bimonthly basis to update your CV, adding any publications, speeches or presentations you have made either on- or off-campus in the previous few weeks, names of your new graduate students and other graduate students whose committees you have been asked to join, courses you have taught, and so on. You also need to organize hard copies (and electronic copies, where possible) of your published papers so you can retrieve them at a moment's notice.

Such a system is only effective, of course, if you actually respond to the reminder from your computer or PDA and take the hour or so every couple of months that is needed to keep your record of accomplishments up to date. Of course, if you are fortunate enough to have a Personal Live Assistant to help with record keeping—an administrative assistant, for example—you are in an even better position. People tend to be much better naggers than electronic devices: you can't just hit them on the head in order to get them to

- In addition to the most obvious scholarships and grants, find out what else you may be eligible for. Many grants and scholarships are not widely advertised. Some of them may be financed by private companies as well as by government or educational institutions.

- Whether you are planning a career in academics or not, you can build your CV, your knowledge, and your circle of contacts by joining committees that include faculty. Say "Yes" to opportunities related to your academic interests. (In particular, welcome any opportunity you are offered to sit on a review panel or any kind of selection committee. The experience you will gain from contributing to deliberations that involve choosing one excellent candidate over another will give you invaluable insights into the kinds of challenges faced by reviewers at funding agencies.)

- Try to get published during graduate school. Ask for help to make it happen. Even if you are not successful, writing articles teaches you how to convey your thoughts in a logical fashion, which helps with future grant or scholarship applications as well as future writing projects. And if you are successful, a publication is a tremendous credential toward the next stage of your career.

stop pestering you. Again, however, you must take the initiative to establish a system so that your assistant understands that focusing on your CV is an important part of your work and that reminding you to do that is part of his or her responsibility.

Related Documents

Particularly as your CV grows in length, you will want to create several additional documents that will be of tremendous use in preparing funding applications. (These documents are useful in other situations, too, such as when you need to give notes to someone who will be introducing you as a speaker.) It is worth it to take a day at some point to create, and then half a day once or twice a year to update, these complementary documents.

- *CV summary.* This is a condensed version of your CV, ten to twelve pages in length, for use in situations where the entire one hundred or even twenty-five pages may be inappropriately long. A CV summary that includes the highlights to date and/or most recent accomplishments can save you hours of effort when a deadline looms for a submittal in which you are permitted to send in a CV of a limited number of pages. If you have such a document prepared ahead of time, you retain control of it, working in the calm light of day to see that it reflects the range and depth of your achievements. Condensing your CV at the last minute is sure to result in a less-than-satisfactory summary of your work.

- *Most important career contributions to date.* This list should include a minimum of five and a maximum of ten achievements and should be no longer than one page. It generally includes books and significant work published in respected journals, with a statement following each entry to explain its significance. For example, an entry might say, "Tested six high-speed superconducting x-ray calorimeters, demonstrating their potential applications in the semi-conductor industry." It may also include such entries as elections, appointments, and awards.

- *A biography.* This, too, should be limited to one page—or even one paragraph. This is an encapsulation in prose of the work you have done in your field. It is suitable as the basis for an author's note in a book or other publication, or for your profile in a conference program where you are giving an address, as well as for an investigator's biography in a funding application.

- *Nonacademic contributions.* Do not overlook the work you do in your home community: fundraising for the local playground, performing in community theater, chairing the regional Little League Baseball program. Such contributions are also easily lost to memory over time, and they may not be suitable to include in an academic CV. You should keep track of them somewhere, perhaps in an entirely separate file—for your own satisfaction when you reflect back on your life at the age of ninety, but also in case you ever decide to run for office, or should someone decide to nominate you for a nonacademic award such as the Congressional Gold Medal, the Order of Canada, or the Order of the British Empire.

✎ Archive It

Make sure that your CV and all related files are effectively backed up on your computer and stored as hard copy in at least two separate physical locations. ▮

Why Bother Keeping Track?

Just as it is necessary to get yourself into an appropriate mindset in order to write an effective funding application—which, as we discussed earlier, you do in part by reminding yourself of the spin-off benefits of doing such work—you need to think of personal record keeping as an essential aspect of career building rather than as a chore. Again, it is a matter of control. If you have taken the necessary steps in a time of quiet reflection to ensure that all your accomplishments are recorded and presented in the most effective way possible, you can feel confident in the accuracy and completeness of the resulting document, and it will be available whenever you need to use it.

Such documents also contribute to building confidence in general. The very act of sitting down regularly to reread and reconsider your achievements can have a long-term positive effect on self-esteem. Having your "lifeboat" ready is especially useful during times of stressful committee work, when people from other divisions make you forget you even have a discipline of your own and have done something to advance knowledge in your field. (If those committees get too stressful, an updated CV can also be an important tool in your efforts to find a more satisfying position somewhere else.)

Most relevant to the subject of this book, of course, having your CV and related documents prepared ahead of time will save you hours of frustration (and possibly panic) when it is time to prepare a funding application, either as the principal investigator or as a member of a team. As we have seen throughout this book, creating such applications is a time-consuming process. Therefore, the more you have done ahead of time, the better: the last thing you need the night before a deadline, when the application is all but done, is to still have the job of updating and then cutting forty pages out of your CV.

Adding to Your Credentials

Keeping a firm grip on the list of your accomplishments will serve you well in terms of recording the past, and it can also spur you onward to initiatives that will help you to increase the impact of your work. In addition to publications and presentations, keep in mind two other important acknowledgments of what you have accomplished: nominations for awards and prizes, and nominations for fellowship in scholarly societies. These kinds of achievement will be of particular value to scholars who are raising their funding focus toward more challenging competitions.

When it comes to prizes and fellowships, often it is necessary for you to nudge the process into life, because your colleagues are likely to be too busy to think of nominating you for anything. A well-placed suggestion with the research chair of your department or a senior member of the academic staff who thinks highly of your work can have excellent results. Your university may have a designated awards facilitator but, if not, an experienced member of the research office staff can often help.

It is hard for some people to overcome the modesty their parents drummed into their heads when it comes to putting themselves forward for awards and prizes for which they are, in fact, eligible. If you are feeling shy about blowing your own horn, reflect on these considerations:

- If you do not help to initiate a nomination, and no one else does anything, you run the risk of turning bitter as you approach retirement when you reflect that you have never even been nominated for several significant awards that you might easily have captured.

- Winning awards and prizes reflects well on your university, college, faculty, department, research center, and elsewhere, as well as on yourself, so you are really being nominated (and, it is to be hoped, winning) for other people's sake as well as your own. The funding development office, for example, is going to love you—as will the communications department.

- Any fear you may experience in regard to the downsides of achieving excellence (these may arise in some of the petty arenas of academe and include ostracism and other forms of emotional abuse) can be easily overcome with a few moments of reflection on the satisfaction you will feel in outdistancing small-minded colleagues, and of the great celebration you will be able to enjoy with those who embrace, understand, and support what you are doing with your talents.

Awards and Prizes

There are many awards, prizes, fellowships, and funded chairs and memberships for which one can apply or be nominated. These honors recognize scholarly achievement and often help to extend and sustain it with additional funds. Many universities and colleges maintain databases of such honors which can be accessed by anyone. Locate relevant databases by searching such key words and phrases as "awards database scholars," "awards database chemistry," "awards prizes neurophysiology research," and so on.

What awards and prizes are you eligible for right now? What are the parameters of the awards and prizes for which you may become eligible in the future? It's a good idea to create a list of possibilities, short and long term. Many researchers and scholars find it beneficial to start "small," by working toward a discipline-specific prize for new researchers, for example, or a distinguished researcher award from their home university (especially if they are on the faculty of a small or moderate-sized institute or institution). Acquiring such credentials will add heft to your nomination package when you move into the larger leagues. By studying the successful nominees for awards and prizes, you can gain a sense of the attributes that awards panels value—such as experience on disciplinary association committees, for example.

Rather than always looking back at your achievements to see whether you are eligible for any awards or prizes, try looking forward and grooming yourself to become eligible to win them. ▌

Developing outstanding nominations for awards and prizes is as difficult and time consuming as developing outstanding submissions for grants, and the methodology is almost identical, so this book can serve as a guide for developing awards nominations as well as for funding applications. The only major difference between the two types of proposal is who sits on the committees that are established to prepare them. For nominations for awards and prizes, the following people need to be involved:

- the nominee (unless the prize is confidential, of course, but in that case the nomination procedure will not concern you at all anyway—or at least not visibly);
- the nominator;
- an administrator, preferably someone with editorial skills who can do the legwork, set deadlines, contact referees, and ensure

that all support documents and letters are in order. This person should be someone who can contact the foundation or organization that is offering the award, seeking clarifications on any points if necessary. The person ought to be able to serve as an objective and frank bystander, giving you feedback so neither you nor your nominator uses unsubstantiated superlatives on the one hand, or undercuts or deemphasizes your achievements on the other.

Societies and Fellowships

Most academic disciplines have national and international societies that provide a variety of services to members, such as:

- encouraging critical thinking and discussion in the field through meetings, workshops, and publications;
- serving as the representative of academics in the discipline to schools, libraries, and the public;
- assuming an advocacy role with governments, funding agencies, and policymakers; and
- generally nurturing excellence.

Quite aside from the benefits that accrue from the opportunity to meet and work with individuals in related fields from other institutions, membership in such organizations is a service that scholars can perform in order to support newer scholars and to contribute to a positive public perception of their field. Those who aspire to win awards and prizes and even in some cases to secure specific funding often find it useful to join such organizations if for no other reason than to be able to add their memberships to their CVs.

A further advantage to membership in these societies is that one becomes eligible for a range of prizes and awards that are specifically directed at those who have achieved distinction in the discipline, not least of which is the opportunity to be nominated for society fellowship. Those who have been elevated by their peers to the status of "fellow" may number in some cases among less than 0.5 percent of the society's total membership (for example, in the case of the American Physical Society), so the distinction becomes a sign of preeminence and carries significant weight with funding-agency reviewers and others.

Most countries also have honorific societies in the health and life sciences, the natural sciences, the social sciences, and the humanities (or in some cases a combination of these); for these societies, election is a requirement of membership. Well-known examples are the National Academy of Sciences and the American Academy of Arts and Letters in the United States, the five academies of the Institut de France (including the Académie Française), the Royal Society of London and the Royal Society for the Encouragement of Arts, Manufactures and Commerce (RSA) in Great Britain, and the Royal Society of Canada. Many learned societies elect international members as well as scholars from their own countries.

When you think about being nominated for national or international societies, you need to anticipate a long lead time, involving the submission of a range of support documents, the solicitation of letters of reference from highly distinguished researchers in your field, and the active support of colleagues from your home institution or other colleagues who have already been elected fellows of the society. Most nominees are not elected to fellowship in societies the first year of their nomination, but if you help your nominators to keep your documents current and effective, your combined efforts can produce valuable results in the long term.

The Upward Spiral

For all kinds of applications and nominations—for grants, for awards and prizes, and for fellowship in scholarly societies—the overall career plan is to start small and grow. We all know people who have burst suddenly into the limelight, winning an international research award before being elected to fellowship in their national society. But in far greater numbers are those who have steadily pursued excellence in their field of study, seeking publication in increasingly prestigious journals instead of setting their sights low and safe, making the effort to network with outstanding scientists from around the world, training excellent scholars who will carry on their work well into the future, and conducting outstanding research—thanks to funding awarded on the basis of their exceptional funding applications.

With a solid plan for developing stature, and care with all of the support issues that contribute to a solid career in academe, you greatly enhance the possibility of a highly successful outcome.

THERE'S A SAYING THAT "luck is for the unprepared." While this statement cannot be taken at face value, it is true that if you have followed some or all of the recommendations for creating an effective funding application that you have read in this book, you have reduced the need for good fortune to shine upon you. However much or little luck you still require, I wish that amount to you.

APPENDIX A
Sample Research Proposal

....

This appendix presents a sample research proposal two ways: first in a "wrong" way, and then in a more effective way. (The proposal is for an invented research program carried out by five imaginary investigators.) The wrong way, Version 1, contains many errors, omissions, and structural infelicities—many more than most proposals submitted to a funding agency would actually contain. Seeing the range of mistakes that appear in Version 1 will help you spot (or avoid) similar problems in your own proposal.

Version 1 appears in two forms: as an unmarked draft, labeled "Version 1," and as "Version 1 Annotated," which contains my comments within [square brackets]. Reading Version 1 will help you test your own abilities to spot errors. You may want to make notes on the unmarked draft and compare them with my comments in Version 1 Annotated.

The second time the proposal is presented, Version 2, the errors have been corrected, the writing has been improved, and the ideas have been clarified. Version 2 is more effective partly because it is more straightforward and structured but also because it does not contain distracting and annoying errors and inconsistencies.

VERSION 1

The Use of Distraction to Manage Pain

Introduction

The four investigators involved in this study represent a unique interdisciplinary team that brings together experienced researchers from a range of backgrounds. They combine outstanding expertise in pain management, trauma care, psychology, and computers in order to advance the status of scientific knowledge regarding the non-pharmacologic control of pain.

B. Gudonov, PhD, the study's PI, is a professor in the Department of Psychology at Research University in University City. He is a senior editor at the *Journal of Acute Care Psychology,* and has published in *J. of Consulting Psych* and *Trauma Psych Bulletin.* Although his primary area of focus in the has been on the ways in which patients respond to withdrawal of pain medications as their wounds or injuries heal, in committee work with John Doe, RN, PhD, Dr. Gudonov became interested in how pain might be managed in non-pharmacologic ways in the emergency room, and this combined with reading he had done into the potential for computer games to become addictive was the genesis of the current study.

P. W. Grimes, MD, FACS, FAEEP has been an emergency-care specialist for nearly twenty years, and her position as Director of Emergency Care at Research University Hospital (RUH) in University City has contributed to her particular interest in the impact of facilities management on emergency care. E. A. Onegin, MD, PhD, FACOEP, director of the RUH Center for Pain Management, brings a strong background in anesthesiology and pain management to the current project, with a specific focus on pain in trauma patients who may ultimately require surgery. J. R. Doe, PhD, RN, CEN, CCRN is an emergency-care nurse, an associate professor of emergency- and trauma-care nursing at Research University, and associate director of the RUH Center for Pain Management. J. M. Tosca, PhD, is an assistant professor at the Puccini Institute of Technology in nearby Sutton. Her particular interests involve cognitive sciences and human factors in computer systems, with a particular emphasis on developing interfaces for games that contribute to learning in individuals with cognitive impairments such as FAS and ADD. Her papers have appeared in *J Ed Tech* and *Neuroscience,* and she has spoken on computer learning at educational conferences around the world.

There are increasingly long wait periods in emergency facilities in hospitals throughout the United States (Smucker, 1995). In an earlier study, Gudonov et al. (2004) showed that the average time between admission and consultation with a physician in the emergency department at RUH in University City is between three and four hours. In non-life-threatening circumstances, the wait for x-rays and to see a physician can extend up to 12 hours and even longer. In some hospitals, many patients essentially become "boarders" in the hospital hallways (Mark and Solway, 2006) and this is beginning to happen at RUH as well. Several efforts to reduce this time at RUH based on findings elsewhere (including admitting patients from emergency more promptly to medical and surgical units and diverting ambulances during times of high emergency-unit use) has not significantly reduced the wait.

In mild to moderately severe emergency situations (e.g., limb fractures), hospital protocols at RUH do not allow nonmedical staff to administer medications to control pain prior to assessment by qualified physicians, due to potential impairment of the patient's ultimate ability to explain his or her condition to the physician when s/he does arrive, and the potential conflict with anesthesia should surgery be required. It is therefore necessary for patients to remain in the emergency waiting room and then the emergency cubicle, unmedicated and often in considerable pain, for up to several hours.

The purpose of the current research is to investigate whether distraction through the use of computer games can make the stay before seeing an emergency room physician "seem" less long and less painful.

Literature Review

Very little research has been undertaken as to the efficacy of computer games as a method of distraction in emergency units with adult patients. Dentists have used televisions to distract patients for years, in part to reduce awareness of pain, but also to control the behavior of children (Smart, 2001). Indeed, numerous studies into the use of distraction among pediatric patients in medical contexts have been undertaken as well, and it has frequently been noted that children receive pain medication less often than adults in general (Johns and Johns, 2006, 2004). However, there is strong evidence that distraction does help in the management of pain (Jacoby and Billingsgate, 2005).

The Study

University Hospital in Research City and two other emergency units serve a predominately middle-class suburban population of half a million people, with approximately five hundred visiting the RUH emergency unit each week. As previously mentioned, there is typically a five-hour wait to see a physician.

The RUH emergency unit is basically an open area with curtains that create up to twenty cubicles when closed. For the current study, computer screens will be hung from anchored metal frames in the ceiling in one half (n = 10) of the cubicles. Three types of games will be available on these computers, based on types and elements that have been determined to be appropriate to adults and older children, and generating high interest among the widest segment of the population. One game will be very simple, easy to learn (modeled on PacMan) for those without computer experience. One will be an adventure-based game for those with more sophisticated interests in computer games. The third game will be knowledge based (e.g., a trivia-type game, or a word game). It is worth nothing that none of the games will not require sound, so as not to disturb staff or patients in cubicles nearby.

Patients who have been assigned to one of the cubicles with computer monitors will be offered a game controller, and invited to play any of the three games while they wait.

Dr. Tocsa will be in charge of this aspect of the research. She has spent five years (Tosca, 2004, 2005, and 1007) conducting qualitative research into the relationships among learning, ease of computer interface, and user engagement.

Design

The study will be qualitative, phenomenological in nature, primarily consisting of closed-answer questions. The data-gathering phase will occur between 8 a.m. and 8 p.m. over a period of six weeks. All patients who come to the emergency room by private vehicle or on foot and who are not admitted directly to the hospital but are instead registered and then asked to be seated in the waiting room, will be asked if they are willing to participate in a noninvasive study to help with patient care. They will sign a form to indicate their willingness to participate. Graduate students for all of the investigators will participate. They will be trained as interviewers. We estimate that we are likely to get at least six hundred prospective subjects, of which it is estimated that five hundred will agree to participate (based on previous studies). Willing participants will sign release form. When these individuals are admitted to a cubicle, those assigned (randomly) to a cubicle with a computer screen will be issued with a computer monitor. Every fifteen minutes while they are waiting for the physician to attend, the cubicle will be checked by the graduate student to see whether the game is being played. to its occurrence. All patients leaving cubicles, whether they had a computer game or not, will be asked closed questions ("Estimate the length of time you waited in the cubicle," "How much pain were you in?" etc. See questionnaire, attached.)

[The proposal goes on to discuss plans for dissemination and related research initiatives the investigators envision for the future.]

VERSION I ANNOTATED

The Use of Distraction to Manage Pain

[The title is imprecise. A better title is "Using Video Games as Distractions from Pain in Hospital Emergency Facilities."]

Introduction

[The subtitle "Introduction" is unnecessary. The first section of any written text is assumed by the reader to be the introduction.]

The four investigators involved in this study represent a unique interdisciplinary team that brings together experienced researchers from a range of backgrounds. They combine outstanding [Avoid empty adjectives.] expertise in pain management, trauma care, psychology and computers in order to advance the status of scientific knowledge regarding the non-pharmacologic control of pain. [This paragraph, which tells the reader nothing concrete, can be eliminated.]

B. Gudonov, PhD, the study's PI, is a professor in the Department of Psychology at Research University in University City. [The biographies should be located later in the document—after the reader understands the concept of the proposed investigation. The role of the bios is to help the reviewer understand how the qualifications of the various researchers will contribute to the study.] He is a senior editor at the *Journal of Acute Care Psychology*, and has published in *J. of Consulting Psych* and *Trauma Psych Bulletin*. Although his primary area of focus in the has [Typographical error.] been on the ways in which patients respond to withdrawal of pain medications as their wounds or injuries heal, in committee work with John Doe, RN, PhD, Dr. Gudonov became interested in how pain might be managed in non-pharmacologic ways in the emergency room, and this, combined with reading he had done into the potential for computer games to become addictive, [The word *addictive* may raise alarms. Better phrasing would be "combined with his interest in psychological responses to computer games."] was the genesis of the current study.

P. W. Grimes, MD, FACS, FAEEP has been an emergency-care specialist for nearly twenty years, and her position as Director of Emergency Care at Research University Hospital (RUH) in University City has contributed to her particular interest in the impact of facilities management on emergency care. E. A. Onegin, MD, PhD, FACOEP, director of the RUH Center for Pain Management, brings a strong background in anesthesiology and pain management to the current project, with a specific focus on pain in trauma patients who may ultimately require surgery. [It is not made clear why E. A. Onegin is involved in the research project.] J. R. Doe, PhD, RN, CEN, CCRN is an emergency-care nurse, an associate professor of emergency- and trauma-care nursing at Research University, and associate director of the RUH Center for Pain Management. [If this is a different John/J. Doe from the one cited in the previous paragraph, the fact they they are two separate individuals must be made clear. If they are the same John/J. Doe, then the use of first name/middle initial and the degrees following the last name must be consistent.] J. M. Tosca, PhD, is an assistant professor at the Puccini Institute of Technology in nearby Sutton. Her particular interests involve cognitive sciences and human factors in computer systems, with a particular emphasis on developing interfaces for games that contribute to learning in individuals with cognitive impairments such as FAS and ADD. [Do not use acronyms unless they need to be used repeatedly in the document. These terms should be spelled out to avoid confusion.] Her papers have appeared in *J Ed Tech* and *Neuroscience*, and she has spoken on computer learning at educational conferences around the world. [The reader is now officially bored.]

There are increasingly long wait periods in emergency facilities in hospitals throughout the United States (Smucker, 1995). [This reference is outdated, and the sentence is overly general.] In an earlier study, Gudonov et al. (2004) showed that the average time between admission and consultation with a physician in the emergency department at RUH in University City is between three and four hours. In non-life-threatening circumstances, the wait for x-rays and to see a physician can extend to twelve hours and even longer. [Reference needed.] In some hospitals, many patients essentially become "boarders" in the hospital hallways (Mark and Solway, 2006) and this is beginning to happen at RUH as well. [Irrelevant information.] Several efforts to reduce this time at RUH based on findings elsewhere (including admitting patients from emergency more promptly to medical and surgical units and diverting ambulances during times of high emergency-unit use) has not significantly reduced the wait.

In mild to moderately severe emergency situations (e.g., limb fractures), hospital protocols at RUH do not allow nonmedical staff to administer medications to control pain prior to assessment by qualified physicians, [We hope that all physicians at the hospital are qualified. Focus on what ideas are being communicated as well as on what words are being used.] due to potential impairment of the patient's ultimate ability to explain his or her condition to the physician when s/he does arrive, [The last four words can be deleted without altering the meaning.] and the potential conflict with anesthesia should surgery be required. It is therefore necessary for patients to remain in the emergency waiting room and then the emergency cubicle, unmedicated and often in considerable pain, for up to several hours. [This sentence repeats information provided earlier and needs tightening.]

The purpose of the current research is to investigate whether distraction through the use of computer games can make the stay before seeing an emergency room physician "seem" less long and less painful. [Far too late in the document the writer finally explains the purpose of the research. The word *seem* is overly informal, and the use of quotation marks draws attention to its inappropriateness. The appropriate term for the focus of the study is "patients' perceptions": i.e., "can alter patients' perceptions about the length of time spent before seeing an emergency room physician."]

Literature Review

Very little research has been undertaken [This is another overly vague statement. Do a thorough literature review and then speak with confidence about how this is the first study, or explain how your study differs from other, similar, studies.] as to the efficacy of computer games as a method of distraction in emergency units with adult patients. Dentists have used televisions to distract patients for years, in part to reduce awareness of pain, but also to control the behavior of children (Smart, 2001). Indeed, numerous studies into the use of distraction among pediatric patients in medical contexts have been undertaken as well, and it has frequently been noted that children receive pain medication less often than adults in general [Irrelevant.] (Johns and Johns, 2006, 2004). [Use chronological order unless references cite two different topics, in which case the topics should be individually identified in the text.] However, there is strong evidence that distraction does help in the management of pain (Jacoby and Billingsgate, 2005). [The word *strong* suggests that there will be more than one reference, but only one reference appears.]

The Study

University Hospital in Research City and two other emergency units serve a predominately middle-class suburban population of half a million people, with approximately five hundred visiting the RUH emergency unit each week. As previously mentioned, there is typically a five-hour wait to see a physician. [The reference to a "five-hour wait" is an inconsistency within the document, which previously stated that the wait is between three and four hours.]

The RUH emergency unit is basically an open area with curtains that create up to twenty cubicles when closed. For the current study, computer screens will be hung from anchored metal frames in the ceiling in one half (n = 10) of the cubicles. Three types of games will be available on these computers, based on types and elements that have been determined to be appropriate to adults and older children, and generating high interest among the widest segment of the population. [This sentence repeats the word *types* and uses too many words to make its point.] One game will be very simple, easy to learn (modeled on PacMan) for those without computer experience. One will be an adventure-based game for those with more sophisticated interests in computer games. The third game will be knowledge-based (e.g., a trivia-type game, or a word game). It is worth nothing ["Worth nothing" rather than "worth noting" is a significant typographical error that changes the meaning significantly.] that none of the games will not ["Not" is another typo which also changes the meaning.] require sound, so as not to disturb staff or patients in cubicles nearby.

Patients who have been assigned to one of the cubicles with computer monitors will be offered a game controller, and invited to play any of the three games while they wait.

Dr. Tocsa [The name is spelled wrong; see the third paragraph in the proposal, above, and the references that follow, below.] will be in charge of this aspect of the research. She has spent five years (Tosca, 2004, 2005, and 1007) [The year should be 2007. Dates and other numbers must be checked especially carefully.] conducting qualitative research into the relationships among learning, ease of computer interface, and user engagement.

Design

The study will be qualitative, phenomenological in nature, primarily consisting of closed-answer questions. The data-gathering phase will occur between 8 a.m. and 8 p.m. over a period of six weeks. All patients who come to the emergency room by private vehicle or on foot and who are not admitted directly to the hospital but are instead registered and then asked to be seated in the waiting room will be asked if they are willing to participate in a noninvasive study to help with patient care. They will sign a form to indicate their willingness to participate.

Graduate students for all of the investigators will participate. They will be trained as interviewers. [It is not made clear how training graduate students will advance their expertise as researchers and scholars. There is a need here to show that the students will not be used as cheap labor.] We estimate that we are likely to get at least six hundred prospective subjects, [Needs a reference.] of which it is estimated that five hundred will agree to participate (based on previous studies). [Needs a reference.] Willing participants will sign a release form. [Repeats information from previous paragraph.] When these individuals are admitted to a cubicle, those assigned (randomly) to a cubicle with a computer screen will be issued with a computer monitor. Every fifteen minutes while they are waiting for the physician to attend, the cubicle will be checked by the graduate student to see whether the game is being played. to its occurrence. [A sentence fragment left over from a previous draft?] All patients leaving cubicles, whether they had a computer game or not, will be asked closed questions ("Estimate the length of time you waited in the cubicle," "How much pain were you in?" etc. See questionnaire, attached.)

[The proposal goes on to discuss plans for dissemination and related research initiatives the investigators envision for the future.]

VERSION 2

Using Video Games as Distractions from Pain in Hospital Emergency Facilities

Long waits for care have become the norm in emergency facilities across the country, particularly for patients whose medical needs are immediate but not life-threatening. Due to hospital protocols many of these patients must wait until they have seen a physician before they are able to receive any medication for their pain. The purpose of this interdisciplinary qualitative study is to determine whether the use of video games can alter patients' perceptions about the length of time that elapses before they see an emergency room physician. The investigators do not intend this intervention to be a long-term solution to waiting times in hospitals, but rather a potential short-term option that may also teach us something about the role of distraction in pain management.

University Hospital in Research City and two other emergency units serve a predominately middle-class suburban population of half a million people, with approximately five hundred individuals visiting the RUH emergency unit each week. Patients typically wait three to four hours to see a physician (Gudonov, 2005). Three of the investigators in the current study are based at the RUH, and two are active in the hospital's pain management center. The fourth investigator is a computer education specialist based in a nearby city.

The literature review was undertaken in four parts. First we assessed recent studies relating to the management of wait times in emergency facilities at similarly sized hospitals. [Cite relevant findings, in logical order.] We then reviewed the literature pertaining to the use of distraction in the management of pain. [Cite relevant findings, in logical order.] We then investigated . . . [Complete the literature review section, including not only the pain-management studies, but also those associated with the computer-game component. This background information will allow reviewers to assess the need for the study].

The current study will be a phenomenological investigation into perceptions of pain and the passage of time by patients in the RUH emergency facility in University City. The study will involve a questionnaire that solicits patient feedback by means of closed-ended questions (see questionnaire, attached). Questionnaires obtained from those who are offered computer games will be compared to questionnaires obtained from those not offered a distraction.

[Proposal goes on in a logical manner to set out the methodology to be used, the nature of the analysis, how graduate students will be involved, and how the findings will be disseminated. It concludes with a summary of future research-related directions or implications for implementation that may be taken, depending on the results. Appended to the document is the questionnaire and a list of all references cited in the proposal, followed by the biographies of the investigators. Every item in the budget is connected to the proposal.]

APPENDIX B

Sample Project Summary

···

The following project summary (also known as the project "abstract") sets out all of the elements of the proposed research in less than two hundred words. The language is straightforward enough that a nonspecialist can understand the intent of the research, but the description also assumes basic knowledge on the part of its expert readers—for example, the expert reader will be familiar with terms such as *transgenic plants* and *standard molecular biological methods of DNA hybridization*. The summary provides context (by clarifying the relevance of the proposed study to the larger picture), it describes the innovative nature of the study, and it explains the appropriateness of the environment in which the research will take place.

LENTIL HYBRIDIZATION TO INCREASE IRON CONTENT
(PI: JM Burnaby, PhD, University City Center for Agricultural Research)

Lentils (*Lens culinaris*) are the source of a range of nutrients that contribute to human health. Their iron content, which is the highest of any vegetable, provides particular value to humans—especially women—who maintain vegetarian diets. Northwestern regions in North America are becoming major producers of lentils, with Invented Lentil No. 1 being the most easily grown in the temperate climate of the Northwest and increasingly popular with consumers. Invented Lentil No. 2, indigenous to semi-arid areas in subtropical climates, has a marginally higher iron content (3.9g/100g vs. 3.5g/100g) but requires a longer growing season to produce an equivalent crop volume. The purpose of the current study is to hybridize Invented Lentil No. 1 with Invented Lentil No. 2 over a period of ten growing seasons with the goal of decreasing the period required for the plant to reach maximum seed-bearing maturity, while increasing the iron content. Researchers in the award-winning facilities of the University City Seed Center will use standard molecular biological methods of DNA hybridization to generate the transgenic plants. Their objective will be to maintain inbred mechanisms for disease control while increasing the iron content in lentils appropriate for cultivation in northwestern regions of North America.

APPENDIX C

Effective Letters of Support

....

You might wish you could send this appendix to the people who have agreed to write letters of reference on your behalf. On the other hand, doing so might be seen as an insult to those people, many of whom are senior to you in age and experience or are significantly advanced in terms of achievements in your field. The very people you are most likely to want to write letters for you are also those you least want to insult.

In most cases you will never know the contents of the letters you so carefully solicited because, in order to maintain the integrity of the funding process, most agencies ask writers to submit their letters directly to the agency, under separate cover from your application. Many otherwise excellent candidates are forever unaware that their applications were unsuccessful not because of any defects in the proposals but because of deficiencies in their "support" letters. Such deficiencies are occasionally intentional, but more often they are simply caused by the writer's inability to compose a decent letter or to give appropriate attention to the task.

If you have any doubts about whether the person you are asking to support you is actually a supporter of your work, it is wise to phrase your initial solicitation in a way that addresses any potential lack of enthusiasm. You could say, for example, "I would be very grateful if you would agree to write this letter of support on my behalf, but if for any reason you feel uncomfortable with this request or are perhaps too busy, please let me know, and I will willingly ask someone else." If you fail to clear the air beforehand, some senior scholars will view their roles as "references" quite liberally—and may poke all the holes they can find in your research program in order to advance the cause of science as a whole.

Even dedicated supporters of your work are sometimes distracted by their own achievements, which causes them to feel that a letter of support for you should really focus primarily on them. Others are simply ineffectual writers who do not realize that a good support letter neither damns with faint praise nor speaks in generalities. The review panel attempting to assess your application will not be helped by lukewarm testimonials such as "My experiences in working with the candidate have generally been positive."

If you are fortunate, your letter writers will ask if there is anything in particular you would like them to stress in the letters of support. If so, spend some time thinking about which of your strengths and accomplishments you would like them to emphasize.

You can exert a small amount of control on the outcome of the letter-writing initiative by providing a modicum of uninvited direction when you extend your original invitation. You can say, for example,

> I am writing to ask whether you would consider writing a letter of reference for my application to the National Science Foundation for funding to support the second phase of my investigation into the olfactory capacity of *Colomba livia* and its implications for species management. I am attaching the statement that summarizes the project I intend to carry out with this funding, and a preliminary budget. I would be grateful if you would speak particularly to my capacity to complete the work effectively, and how my investigations may contribute to our knowledge of Columbidae specifically and to the management of birds that may pose health risks to humans in urban settings more generally.

When *you* are asked to write letters of support, here are some things you can do to craft a useful letter of reference.

- Introduce yourself in the first paragraph. Mention the credentials you have that make you qualified to write the letter.
- Say how you know the applicant and under what circumstances

you are familiar with the applicant's work or work habits. (Conflicts of interest or lack thereof should be stated.)

- Comment specifically on the potential benefits of the current study or project. State how the proposed research will advance scholarship in the field that you share with the applicant.
- Include other relevant observations about the study's intellectual rigor, the applicant's dedication, vision, and potential, or comparisons (if positive) to (unnamed) others with whom the writer has worked who were at similar stages in their academic careers.
- Indicate why the world in general could use more information about this issue at this particular time (the big picture).
- Comment on the potential benefits of the research to the development of highly qualified personnel in the field.

Do not write beyond the length requested by the agency in a reference letter. Just like with the funding application itself, letters of support that extend beyond the permitted length limits may not be forwarded to the review committee.

ANNOTATED BIBLIOGRAPHY

··

These resources provide information on topics related to creating effective funding applications. I have included the resources that I find most useful and accessible. There are, of course, many others.

Many university, college, and funding-agency websites provide specific guidance on grant writing for different categories of research or for particular funding "targets." Graduate-office websites also offer excellent guides to available resources. A search of the Internet with key words that relate to your specific area of investigation or scholarship will produce other leads that you can follow up. Be careful not to follow up on too many (see under "Procrastination," below).

PREPARING FUNDING APPLICATIONS

Proposals That Work: A Guide for Planning Dissertations and Grant Proposals, 5th ed., by L. A. Locke, W. W. Spirduso, and S. J. Silverman. Thousand Oaks, CA: Sage, 2007.

Of particular interest to graduate students but with useful information for all researchers and scholars, this book explains how to plan, organize, and develop your research proposal and how to present your ideas. The authors cover such critical subjects as honesty and ethics in research and writing, how to select a research topic, how to form a committee, common problems in developing research proposals, what the proposal should contain, how to do a thorough literature review, the role of consultants, and oral presentations. The authors also suggest ways to find grants to fund student research, and they discuss scholarships and fellowships. The book includes sample proposals with commentaries.

How to Write a Successful Research Grant Application: A Guide for Social and Behavioral Scientists, edited by W. Pequegnat and E. Stover. New York: Plenum, 1995.

Both halves of the double-barreled title of this book are inaccurate—the first suggesting a wider scope than the book in fact encompasses, the second indicating a narrower potential audience than it has the prospect of assisting. The collection is based on papers presented at a 1990 workshop sponsored by the National Institute of Mental Health (NIMH) in Washington to encourage more funding applications from minority investigators on projects relating to AIDS- and HIV-related research. Several of the chapters are subject specific and out of date. But these negatives are offset by chapters that are of perennial relevance to grant writers, regardless of their field. These include a chapter that focuses on developing exciting (as opposed to boring) hypotheses, one that deals with setting up research questions and hypotheses, and another that looks at grant writing from the perspective of the funding agency. As a bonus, there is a chapter that describes how to deliver an interesting scientific talk.

Grant Application Writer's Handbook, by L. Reif-Lehrer. Boston: Jones and Bartlett, 1995.

This is one of several available books written with a specific focus on the steps required to complete a grant proposal for the National Institutes of Health (NIH) in the United States. Another is *Guide to Effective Grant Writing: How to Write a Successful NIH Grant Application,* by Otto O. Yang (Springer, 2005). While they include valuable information that could be applied to all funding applications, these books are of particular use to those working on scientific research in the health sciences (especially medical research), and particularly those seeking NIH funding.

LOGICAL THINKING

Logic: A Very Short Introduction, by G. Priest. New York: Oxford University Press, 2000.

To writers of funding applications, this brief and engaging introduction to the principles of logic is probably of more use as a diagnostic tool than as a road map. If you have ever been told that there is a logical error in your thinking, Priest's *Logic* will provide you with a definitive list of faulty forms of thinking, allowing you to identify the specific error you have made—while also giving you tools to make mincemeat of those who have accused you. In this primer to what he acknowledges to be a highly complex subject, Priest does his best (and his best is pretty good) to introduce the average intelligent reader to such topics as how statements can be reduced to symbols and formulae for testing, how assertions can be true and false at the same time, how objects can be transformed into other objects while retaining the substance that defines them—not to mention demonstrating why it can be mathematically sound to put a decision off until tomorrow rather than making it today. In general, however—except to those previously versed in philosophical constructs—this book is much better suited to a vacation than to the twelve hours preceding any kind of deadline.

The Art of Thinking: A Guide to Critical and Creative Thought, 7th edition, by V. R. Ruggiero. New York: Pearson Longman, 2004.

In the four sections of this book, Ruggiero talks about developing thinking skills and expanding your perspectives; the creative process, and how to challenge yourself creatively; the role of criticism, and how to refine your thinking and evaluate your arguments; and communication—persuading others and writing well. At the end of each chapter there are exercises of increasing difficulty. Chapter 12, "Evaluate Your Argument on the Issue," may be particularly useful for those who have received criticism about their underlying thinking. An appendix is specifically devoted to the fundamentals of logic.

A Rulebook for Arguments, 3rd ed., by A. Weston. Indianapolis: Hackett Publishing, 2000.

Weston has created a clear and useful guide to the common principles upon which sound arguments are constructed. His rules are numbered (in a logical order, needless to say) so that teachers can simply refer students to Rule #9 ("Use representative examples") or Rule #23 ("Causes may be complex") rather than writing out explanations of specific transgressions. While this book is intended for writers who are developing and evaluating arguments in expository essays and debates, it will be useful to anyone attempting to build a written case for anything. Weston's precision with language and his dexterity with illustrative examples demonstrate his own basic principle that clear writing is as important as sound thinking.

WRITING WELL

Numerous style guides have been published for writers of all types of prose, from nonfiction books and articles to business letters to short stories. Several valuable handbooks have been created specifically for the world of academic writing and publishing, and some have become the standard for style in various disciplines—for example, the *Publication Manual of the American Psychological Association.* The *APA Manual,* as it is called, is the style reference for many books and journals in the health professions and social sciences. It sets guidelines for everything from punctuation to the hierarchy of text headings to the layout of reference pages—and a host of other matters.

Ask the colleagues you respect for their advice and guidance regarding style manuals relevant to your discipline, particularly when it comes to proper formats for laying out articles and developing abstracts, figures, tables, reference lists, and bibliographies.

For general information about writing and formatting, I recommend the following resources, which are two of the essential components of any writer's library.

The Chicago Manual of Style, 15th ed., edited by the University of Chicago Press Staff. Chicago: University of Chicago Press, 2003.

Considered the authority on all matters relating to writing and publishing by most publishers, editors, and professional writers in North America and beyond, *The Chicago Manual of Style* contains information on every step of the writing and publishing process. First published in 1906, it is updated regularly to reflect changes in language and society, and it is highly "user friendly" when it comes to hunting down what you need to know. Chapter titles include "Grammar and Usage," "Punctuation," "Mathematics in Type," "Rights and Permissions," "Manuscript Editing," among others. *The Chicago Manual of Style* is available online by subscription as well as in book and CD-ROM formats.

The Elements of Style, 4th ed., by W. Strunk Jr. and E. B. White. Boston: Allyn and Bacon, 2000.

William Strunk Jr. taught English at Cornell University at the start of the twentieth century. He was determined that his students master the stylistic rules he considered essential to good communication, along with a number of basic rules of spelling and grammar. The course he taught led to the publication of a small book called *The Elements of Style.* One of Strunk's students was E. B. White, who became a noted essayist and author of *Charlotte's Web, Stuart Little,* and many other books. Midcentury, White decided that Strunk's book should be revised and updated, which he did with élan, and the book has been revised and updated again for republication several times since. It is a delight to read and use, not to mention a reliable resource when it comes to figuring out the difference between "disinterested" and "uninterested," knowing how to form a possessive when the name of the subject ends in "s," identifying words that can and should be cut, and understanding the components of an effective sentence.

PROCRASTINATION

Procrastination: Why You Do It, What to Do about It, by J. B. Burka and L. M. Yuen. Cambridge, MA: Perseus, 1983.

Burka and Yuen are practicing psychologists who have studied procrastination and helped people who suffer from it. They describe the symptoms of procrastination and the havoc it can wreak, with the help of examples and case histories, and then propose methods for overcoming such behaviors. The book includes a helpful chapter on living and working with procrastinators.

"Are You a Procrastinator?" by the Procrastination Research Group, Carlton University, Ottawa (http://http-server.carleton.ca/~tpychyl/prg/self_help/self_help_links.html)

The Procrastination Research Group, headed by Professor Tim Pychyl in the Department of Psychology at Carlton University, is an international network of researchers studying a range of issues related to procrastination. In addition to summarizing recent papers and books on the subject, the website provides an entire section for procrastination sufferers and includes information on self-help techniques as well as intervention. There is an emphasis on academic procrastination on this site.

It's about Time: The Six Styles of Procrastination and How to Overcome Them, by L. Sapadin with J. Maguire. New York: Penguin, 1996.

Linda Sapadin is a clinical psychologist with many years of experience in treating patients with procrastination histories that range from the annoying to the life-threatening. She has identified six types of procrastinators (The Perfectionist, The Dreamer, The Worrier, The Defier, The Crisis-Maker, and The Overdoer). For each, she describes typical behaviors, suggests root causes, presents case histories, and offers management techniques. Eminently readable, the book even includes six questionnaires that will help you diagnose the type of procrastination in the talons of which you are gripped.

INDEX